THE INNER WORK OF THE WARRIOR
A Manual for Embodying Spirit

THE
INNER WORK
OF THE WARRIOR
A Manual for Embodying Spirit

George Breed, PhD

Copyright © 2015 by Anamchara Books, a division of Harding House Publishing Service, Inc. All rights reserved. No part of this publication may be reproduced or transmitted in any form or by any means, electronic or mechanical, including photocopying, recording, taping, or any information storage and retrieval system, without permission from the publisher.

Anamchara Books
Vestal, NY 13850
www.anamcharabooks.com

Printed in the United States of America.

First Printing
9 8 7 6 5 4 3 2 1

IngramSpark 2020 paperback ISBN: 978-1-62524-804-6

Cover art: *The Promise of Peace*, © 2003 Cathy Gazda.

To the Source

*And if ye cannot be saints of knowledge,
then, I pray you,
be at least its warriors.
They are the companions and forerunners
of such saintship.*
—Nietzsche

Contents

Acknowledgements..15
Preface..18

Part 1. My Personal Journey..23
  1. The Cosmic Journey..25
  2. The Martial Journey..28
  3. The Professional Journey...34

Part 2. The Mandala: The Wheel of Keen Weapons..........37
  4. The Wheel of Keen Weapons....................................39
  5. Brief Commentary on the Wheel of Keen Weapons....43

Part 3. The Metaphor: Warriors of Spirit.......................49
  6. The Metaphor of War..51
  7. The Monk-Warrior Metaphor....................................53
  8. Monk and Warrior Paths as One..............................56
  9. Self as Mercenary..60
  10. The Sacred and the Profane....................................62
  11. Warrior of Spirit..64

Part 4. Earth Weapons...67

12. The Weapon of Centering..70
    Keep One-Point
    Finding Center
    Small Bowl of Water
    Head / One-Point Comparison
    Mindfulness of One-Point in Daily Life
    One-Point Walking
    Connecting Heart and One-Point
    Grounding Exercise
    Midline Power
    Stance and Midline: The Earthly Triangle
    Your Centering Practice

13. The Weapon of Mindfulness....................................81
    Deadly States of Mind
    The Full Mind
    The Stopped Mind
    The Led Mind
    Trance Mind
    Trance Dance
    Why-ning and How-ling
    Stance Affects Trance
    Chiltan Posture

Going Out of Your Mind
　　　Presence
　　　Vanquishing Negative Thought
　　　Formal and Informal Practice
　　　Your Mindfulness Practice
14. The Weapon of Relentless Intent..............................101
　　　Relentless Intent and Co-Creation
　　　Mind and Body as One
　　　Hauling the Meat: Just Take the One More Next Step
　　　Diamond Sharp
　　　The Silver Cord
　　　Your Practice of Intent

Part 5. Heaven Weapons..109
15. The Weapon of Opening..112
　　　Contemplation: Living in the Temple
　　　Open Awareness
　　　Galeropia: Clear and Cheerful Vision
　　　Settling Down
　　　Spaces Between Thoughts
　　　Condensing and Expanding
　　　Your Opening Practice

16. The Weapon of Surrendering 120
   To Be Rendered
   Total Abandon
   Drop Your Story
   No Enemy
   In the Soup
   Submission
   Forgiving Is Releasing
   Hands Attaching
   Your Surrendering Practice
17. The Weapon of Compassion 131
   Entering and Blending
   Attention and Interbeing
   Appreciation
   Impeding Compassion
   Giving and Receiving
   Your Compassion Practice

Part 6. Horizon Weapons 141
18. The Weapon of Calm 145
   Flaming and Drowning
   Patterns of Anger
   Waiting

    Mind Like Moon, Mind Like Water
    Calm Illumination
    Mothers and Cousins of Calm
    In-Hell-ing and Ex-Hale-ing
    Word Fasting
    Developing Calm
    Your Practice of Calm

19. The Weapon of Action 159
    Calling Energy
    Rhythm
    Synchrony
    Separation Rhythm
    The Rhythm of Others
    Catching that Free-Flowing Rhythm
    Your Action Practice

Part 7. The Mystery: Capacity 169
20. The Target: Great Capacity 173
21. Circum Stance 176
    Knotting
    Re-Form-ing, Re-Bell-ing, and Re-Volt-ing
    Afraid of Nothing
    The Fullness of Emptiness

Emptying

Great Capacity

Your Practice for Allowing Capacity

Epilogue...185
Appendix: The Wheel of Ineptness...............................190
Notes and Additional Reading......................................193

Acknowledgements

Great love goes to my mother, Ruth Lane Smith, who, through relying on spirit, has given me two precious gifts: first, a prime example of trusting in the Life Force and the Wellspring(ing) of its source, and second, her invaluable friendship.

I acknowledge my debt to my father who, through abandoning the family, gave impetus to my following of the path of a warrior of spirit.

A deep bow of respect goes to Sensei Tatsuo Shimabuku (Isshinryu Karate) and Sensei Koichi Tohei (Aikido) for their teachings; and to the US Marine Corps and that particular Marine, Clarence Ewing, for aiding my journey on the martial path.

Great appreciation (holding as precious) for each of my karma companions, the bodhisattva gang with whom I've run for lifetimes, in suffering and in celebration. In order of your appearance in this current embodying: Ed Lane, Lena Lane, Ben Breed, Gene Breed, Ginny Stewart, Kathy Aycock, Glenda Rufer, Ron Lynch, Phil Breed, Irma Shepherd, Joan Fagan, Amanda Breed Hanson, Sid Jourard, Bruce Latta, Cindy Kirkeby, Jerry Gunter, Nancy Skeen, Sandy Hill, Terry Chitwood, Amy Breed, Jacques Kelly, Joe Ricci, Mike Schmidt, Joe Night, Tom Reifers, Wu Chien Lem, Bobbie Alsgaard, Willard Lindstrom, Gerry Frank, Donna Breed, Cynthia Knox, Tom Vendetti, Terry Moore, Nancy Vendetti, Boyce McClung, Bob Frumhoff, Betsy Kerr, Joan Enoch, Jon Rudy, Stan Clark, Patrick Martin, Martha Crowley, Ross Hardwick, Carol Nix, Tricia Fortin, and Stacie Flajnik.

Phil Breed is a light in my life (and the lives of many others) as he continues to naturally follow the warrior path.

Donna Breed, a dynamo of warm wit and quiet action, helped me shop for and obtain a good computer (bringing me out of the dark ages), allowing the production of this manuscript.

Amanda Breed Hanson gave direct and loving encouragement as only a daughter can do, as I moved through some of life's agonies during this period of writing and editing.

I ask for blessings on Amy Buckthorpe Breed who knows the deep truth of these words she heard one night: "You have the power to overcome anything."

The great and unexpected gift of the cover art, which opens a place of silent awe and contemplation, and the cover design of this book, flowed out of the soul of Cathy Gazda.

I am indebted to my dharma buddy, Cynthia Knox, for bringing Dharmaraksita's *The Wheel of Sharp Weapons* to my attention.

Great appreciation to Stan Clark, psychologist-healer-musician-wild man-friend, who in sharing many of his ideas in our creative jawing, opened me to the mandala, used in the book, to depict the Wheel of Keen Weapons.

Love to Betsy Kerr, an embodying of relentless compassion and deep and steadfast companionship across the years. You are a true warrior woman and an ongoing inspiration.

Love to my partner Karen, earth walker, mountain hiker, river runner, lover of cats and wild things, who took in this old dog and, through love, taught him a few new tricks, not the least of which that this book could and should be published.

Homage to my spiritual teachers: Jesus, Lao Tzu, and Buddha, who stand and laugh together.

Preface

People have asked me, "George, why use 'warrior' as your metaphor? Doesn't it carry implications that you don't want?"

That question stuck with me. It became my koan—a problem to solve or dissolve. I went through the standard responses:

1. I don't mean warrior in the destructive sense; a warrior is someone who faces and deals with whatever arises.
2. "Warrior" is the metaphor with which I'm familiar, that I've lived—and if others don't use warrior language, they can translate it to their own language.
3. Warriors have a respectable place in the spiritual traditions of various cultures (for example Arjuna in the Hindu Bhagavad Gita; "put on the whole armor of God" [Ephesians 6:11] in the Christian tradition;

Jesus telling his disciples it was time to get a sword [Luke 22:36]; Shaolin warrior-priests).

All these responses are fine and good, as far as they go. But they don't go very far. They continue to reverberate within the confines of the warrior construct itself—and lots of folks don't want to go anywhere near that construct. If they do venture closer, they get uncomfortable using a predator language (as one participant in a workshop put it to me). So I kept chewing on that hard dry nut of a koan: Why warrior? I could just as readily have used "adventurer" or "sojourner" or "intranaut."

Warriors, however, have a structured discipline, a language, specific practices, and written accounts (data) of their experiments in facing and engaging any situation. Only those whose experiments succeeded left records. Warriorship is an exact and an exacting science. In essence, I trust the data.

Warriors of spirit across the ages and across disciplines (martial arts, healing arts, creative arts, spiritual arts, political arts) embody certain qualities. Embodying (deeply practicing) these qualities reduces stress, increases awareness, deepens confidence, and quiets the mind and opens it to creative solutions. Right relationship occurs, and the state known as flow becomes one's lifestyle. This has nothing to do with the violence of external warfare.

I believe the embodying of these warrior qualities is an essential next step in the transformation of human consciousness and in the survival of the human species. Until our consciousness opens to a greater light of awareness, we will continue to foul our nest, to murder each other and entire species, to hate, to live lives of isolated desperation while engrossed in our own reflections.

Practicing the embodying of these qualities of the warrior of spirit expands our capacity and capability. As our capacity opens, more awareness comes. As more awareness comes, our capacity to receive expands. We become co-creators or partners with the Life Force, with Spirit, in this endeavor.

A purpose of this book is to introduce these warrior qualities (you will find they are not strangers) so that you may sit with them, entertain them, try them on for size, and perhaps find that they become you.

The Inner Work of the Warrior is partly a manual with recipes from the warrior community for consciousness transformation. We are the ingredients. This life we are living is both mixing bowl and oven. Our Source provides the right temperature for our baking.

The root of "manual" is *manus* or hand. In a manual, useful information is made handy, near at hand. The value of a manual is, exactly as the name implies, in its use. A manual sitting on a shelf is in a coma, awaiting someone handy to bring it into life. The person bringing a manual to life is simultaneously resurrected. Possibilities are unleashed.

Interacting with a manual, the reader merges with it, bringing into play the focused intent of all creation. Tab A is actually inserted into Slot A. The carburetor is actually adjusted. The recipe is followed. Eggs are broken and stirred. Something new is born. Concepts are combined with direct bodily experience, so that a depth of comprehension is attained. The person's whole brain, the entire embodied being, begins to know. Centering, for example, is no longer an idea or image, a mental projection, an illusion, but a living action, a way of being in the world.

For those who are only reading this manual, you will get some ideas for intellectual banter in your mental foraging. Unless the qualities discussed are already part of your *experience* or unless you perform the experiments, you will not *know* what you read. If you want water rather than a mirage, you must embody the qualities.

Part 1
My Personal Journey

1

The Cosmic Journey

I began to comprehend that there was a vehicle for journeying and dealing with human existence when I was a fledgling, a boy deeply open to understanding life as best I could from the vantage point of life in a small town in the 1940s. We lived in Alabama, separated from Georgia by the Chattahoochee River. This river was not only a stream of water; it was also a river of time. Looking across it, I could see into the future. Georgia was an hour ahead of Alabama.

I knew since early consciousness that the cosmos takes a personal interest in human lives. My concerns narrowed, over time, into a few questions of basic human existence. How is it we trick ourselves into believing that we are separate chunks of matter, alien from the universe, alien from life, alien from nature, alien from each other? How is it that we trance ourselves into alienation, a trance in which we can become so deeply embedded we are willing to die for it? How is it that we sleep so deeply? How is it that we do not awaken? What are the principles, the operating principles of the cosmos, and thus, the principles by which we can live most fruitfully?

As my life streamed past, a practical model for embodying the Life Force (Spirit) of the universe emerged from two major currents. At age twelve, I was lifted into the cosmos. When I was twenty-on, I began the practice of the martial arts in Okinawa.

The cosmic experience came unexpectedly and with startling clarity. No one else was at home that day. Sitting quietly on the living room sofa, I was suddenly transported to a vantage point where I could see the globe of Earth. I remember a moment of fear that I would not be able to breathe in outer space. Something reassured me, and I breathed calmly and quietly. I looked "down" to see my body. I had no body other than the cosmos itself.

The Earth was beautiful. A soft golden light bathed it through and through, surrounding it with a golden glow. I sensed, felt, and heard the harmony of its music. I saw and knew with deep certainty that all on Earth is interrelated and harmoniously connecting. All is one flow. Separation is an illusion.

I do not know how long the experience lasted. At some point, I was sitting on the sofa once again. I told no one. I knew from listening to adult conversations that no one spoke of such things.

2
THE MARTIAL JOURNEY

The second current in my life stream came when I joined the Marine Corps with two express purposes: to see how I fared in the world of warrior males and to go to Japan. I accomplished both.

Karate

Stepping into martial art training on Okinawa in 1959 was a life-transforming experience. Tatsuo Shimabuku was a small, fierce man who inspired Okinawans and Americans to push themselves to the utmost to learn his particular evolution of the martial arts, Isshinryu (the way of one spirit, one heart, and one mind).

Under his direction, we spun and leaped and kicked and punched in the formal katas and free-style sparring. The poured-concrete floor behind his house toughened our bare feet with its wintry cold and summer heat. The body bag on a high chain swung from jump kicks. The makiwara boards embedded in concrete yielded to our pounding fists and elbow slams.

As we worked through the katas, Sensei would make his rounds and periodically kick or punch particular muscle groups to ensure their appropriate toughness. He corrected our breathing, our form, and our stance. Often, while watching our maneuvers, he would sit quietly pounding a large nail into a two-by-four with the calloused flesh of his hand, occasionally stopping to sip some green tea. Though he spoke little, Sensei Shimabuku taught much: quietness and confidence, the rudiments of Zen (though he never used the word), proper breathing, visual imagery, energy flow, stance, fluidity, focus, toughness, and open awareness.

From Sensei Shimabuku I learned of the existence of martial art principles passed down across the centuries. The principles were displayed in his Agena dojo and on the graduation "silks" presented with a belt award. I wanted still more, and so I searched the journals, diaries, sayings, and aphorisms of those who were recognized as proficient in the martial arts. I wished to be able to speak the truths of these arts in succinct meaningful words, words embodying truth, words pointing to deep understandings of reality, words assisting self-cultivation and transformation.

Jujutsu

After returning to the States, I soon linked up with some black belts in jujutsu in Atlanta, Georgia. Their martial way was more circular than karate. When attacked, they would divert the oncoming energy of the attack into a circular motion, add some of their own energy to the circle, and end with the attacker's body slammed into some immovable object.

The jujutsu style of interaction was more polite than Isshinryu. It said, in effect, "since you choose to follow this path of attack, we will assist you on your chosen trip." The end result, however, was equally as devastating: a broken person.

We combined techniques. The attacker was blocked and softened with karate moves, then circulated through the air into a jujutsu bone break or choke hold. We had great fun, but the model fell short of an appropriate means of harmonious communication.

Ki Development

In 1974, at a summer training camp, I was privileged to attend a six-week training program on Ki Development at Fullerton College, California. On the lawn of the Fullerton campus, the teacher, Sensei Koichi Tohei (Aikido practitioner and student of Morihei Ueshiba, the founder of Aikido), asked for five volunteers to attack him. This smiling dancing man moved in flowing circles and spirals in the midst of attackers who were falling and sailing through the air as they rushed toward a target that was no longer there.

I laughed at the spectacle and at the good-natured humor of this sensei who gave the appearance of a Japanese businessman on vacation — grey hushpuppies, blue socks, navy-blue full-cut slacks, and a white open-necked short-sleeved shirt. Sensei Tohei moved gracefully with agile speed and power.

Finally, I had found the martial art model applicable to daily life: the practice of positively grounding openness allowing non-colliding intimacy with a potential adversary. It was neither necessary nor desirable to rip out the other's throat or slam the other's head into the concrete after a full-body throw. I could dance the dance of no-harm-to-you-no-harm-to-me. I could allow the dance to dance the dance.

I began learning Ki (energy) principles and their applications (mind, body, spirit moving as one) from Sensei Tohei that day. A lifelong focus on embodying these principles in daily life led me to the understanding that martial art principles in their ultimate form are the same as healing art and spiritual art principles.

I began doing seminars, workshops, and retreats on the application of martial arts principles to daily life. A simple list of principles was all I had, principles teased from my own training and from the diaries and journals other martial artists left behind. I taught the principles everywhere I could: hospitals, schools, martial art training halls, Indian Health agencies, senior citizen centers, group homes for the developmentally disabled, state fairs, Elderhostels, state and county governments, community mental health centers, behavioral health agencies, churches, and universities. Of course, as I kept teaching and living these principles, they kept refining me. Meanwhile, as they lived through me, they also continued to refine themselves.

I practiced and taught martial arts (from the hard exterior to the soft interior) while continuing to ponder the writings and journals of those who had gone before me. (If you're curious what those were, take a look at the bibliography at the back of the book.) I also studied the spiritual literature from diverse cultures. These readings (with accompanying practices) gave further validation to the understanding that the so-called "martial" principles were in accord with "spiritual" principles, that they described the same reality, the one cosmos.

3

The Professional Journey

My early research as a psychologist was a continuous pursuit of the dynamics of *nonverbal* communication, a study of the expression of the *spirit* in which things were said, rather than the actual words spoken. This quest naturally overlapped with explorations of therapeutic relationships, of the field of healing, and of the reality of the interdependence and interpenetration of all phenomena (mutual co-arising), as evidenced by my own and others' direct experiences.

I began to understand more deeply that those people who were exemplars of expression of spirit were warriors. It didn't matter whether they used words, healing practices, visual art, or the martial arts, they all had the courage and other warrior qualities needed to follow the path of spirit rather than human conventionality.

As a psychologist, I became interested in the writings of Abraham Maslow (peak experiences), William James (cosmic consciousness and mystic experience), Carl Jung (synchronicity), Sid Jourard (transparent self), Kurt Lewin (field theory), Ken Wilber (integral psychology), and Jean Gebser (the evolution of consciousness). I saw that these thinkers' views of the universe confirmed and enhanced the martial principles. As a psychotherapist, I saw that these principles were meaningful and applicable to the daily lives of individuals caught in physical, emotional, interpersonal, mental, and spiritual pain.

All along the journey, the principles continued to shape and refine themselves. Only within the past few years did they begin forming into the present model, four sets of complementary practices arising out of the pulsating heart of Life itself. These eight transformational practices allow a natural loosening of spiritual knots: the cognitive obscurations and emotional habits that create and compose the little separate self with all its demanding poses, anxieties, sufferings, and fears.

Part 2

The Mandala
The Wheel of Keen Weapons

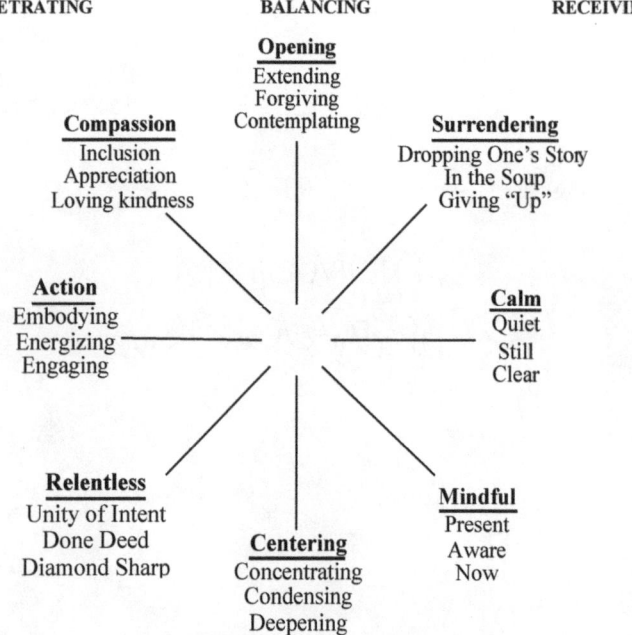

**The Wheel of Keen Weapons:
Practices Promoting
Spiritual Strength**

4

The Wheel of Keen Weapons
Practices Promoting Spiritual Strength

When the early morning sun peeks over the horizon, rays of light flash across the earth. Other rays of the sun are already extending upward into the heavens. This vision of the sun, the heavens, thee, and the horizon forms a wheel of radiant spirit. It is a depiction of eight transformational practices or eight keen weapons of a warrior (see the diagram on the facing page). This "Wheel of Keen Weapons" invites practical embodying of the Life Force, of Spirit in daily life.

If you look at the diagram, you'll see that three of the principles are earth focused: *centering and grounding* while being *mindfully present* with *relentless intent*; three have a Heaven focus: *opening and releasing and forgiving* while *surrendering* with *loving-kindness, compassion, and appreciation*; two are rays of the Horizon: participation in everyday life by being *calm and still* with the speed and rhythm of effective *action*.

When earth and heaven principles are experienced simultaneously, we become like our cousins, the trees. We root and ground ourselves while spreading our branches to the cosmos. This is a practice of great trust. Like trees, we are not destroyed by adversity. No matter the weather, we stand and open to life. With continuing adversity, we extend our roots even deeper, thus being able to open and engage even further.

Like trees "planted by the rivers of water" (Psalm 1:3), we balance the symmetry of our roots with our branches. The deeper and more firmly based our roots are in the Source of our being, the more successfully we engage the wound of this world. Feet on the ground and head in the sky, we are conduits allowing the merging of earthly and heavenly energies. We move back and forth on the horizontal plane conducting our daily business—which is the business of right relationship with all we encounter.

Unlike Dharmaraksita's wheel of sharp weapons, which provides a karmic explanation of our sufferings ("this is the wheel of sharp weapons returning full circle upon us from wrongs we have done"), the Wheel of Keen Weapons represents our opening with full spirit into the world. The work of the Wheel of Keen Weapons effectively engages the soul of the world.

The weapons, the eight warrior qualities, are *keen* weapons. In embodying the qualities, we are the weapons. Keen means not only sharp and acute (having acumen or wisdom), but also bold, daring, fierce, and able. To embody the Wheel of Keen Weapons is to be fiercely alive with the capability and compassion that comes from deep wisdom.

It is no new news that the human race is deeply involved in genocide and suicide. We all play a part in the dinosauric consciousness causing such destruction. We must now step into a new consciousness. A transformation of consciousness is essential for the survival of the human—and many of the nonhuman—species. Embodying the eight warrior qualities produces such a transformation.

To transform our own consciousness requires a continuous practice of stepping out of the mindset that separates reality into pieces. This conceptual layer of divisiveness creates a tendency to harbor suspicion and mistrust. It is an "I"-dolatrous stance of I, I, I and me, me, me. Transformation asks us to continuously practice opening to unitive consciousness. This means identifying with the Source that breathes us. It means regarding daily life as spheres of influence. And it means embodying the radiance of our Source.

The core of the Wheel of Keen Weapons holds space for our Source, the great mystery that gives birth to all without ceasing, with rays of life extending outward. The Source is forever aware and present, eternally grounding and deepening, infinitely opening and releasing. Our Source is inclusionary and compassionate, relentless and intentful, yielding and flexible, calm and still, active and engaging. We are invited to join in, to embody the same characteristics, the same qualities.

The Wheel of Keen Weapons is a model pointing to practices, to a way of being that allows a conscious aligning with our Source, conscious co-creation with God. Embodying the flowering radiance of our Source in daily life—in this world—is our spiritual and evolutionary responsibility.

5

BRIEF COMMENTARY ON THE WHEEL OF KEEN WEAPONS

Earth Practices (Rooting)

- *Centering.* Centering our being before and during any action is essential. Praying is a centering of spirit. So also is settling down to our physical center of balance through a simple intake and slow expulsion of breath.
- *Mindful Presence.* Everything is taking place here in the present immediacy, even the past and the future. Attend to now. Now is the time.
- *Relentless Intent.* We set our face "as a flint." Total commitment, no holding back, the mission has already been accomplished while it is being accomplished.

Heaven Practices (Opening)

- *Opening.* Opening is the counterpart of centering. Once we are centering, we open to all that exists, to

all that is happening. We release apprehension and open to comprehension.
- *Surrendering.* Surrendering to no person, only to our Source, our former way is torn asunder and we are rendered anew. This is a continuous process.
- *Compassion.* Loving-kindness is the partner of relentless intent. We see God in all and all in God. We know it is hard to be meat. We hold appreciation in our hearts.

Horizon Practices (Engaging)

- *Calm.* Calmness allows clear seeing. Embodying the earth and heaven practices produces calmness. We are at home in the universe.
- *Action.* Centering and present with full intent, while also surrendering to God with openness and compassion, we calmly act. What needs to be done is done.

Augmentations

Each practice is augmented or strengthened by the other seven. Each practice is especially strengthened by the two adjacent practices as depicted in the Wheel.

Earth Practices

- The practice of Relentless Intent and Mindfulness strengthens Centering. Centering requires presence, awareness, and living in the Now with diamond-hard, one-pointed intent.
- The practice of Centering and Calm strengthens Mindfulness. Mindful presence requires focusing, condensing, and deepening, while being still, quiet, and clear.
- The practice of Centering while in Action strengthens Relentlessness. Relentless Intent requires the stability of grounding and deepening, while deliberately embodying and calling our energies into engaging life.

Heaven Practices

- The practice of Surrendering and Compassion strengthens Opening. Opening requires surrendering our egos, while extending positive energies outward in all directions without bias (Compassion).
- The practice of Calm and Openness strengthens Surrender. Calm is essential to surrender, which cannot exist within an agitated state, and so is Openness: we surrender into the openness of our Source.

- Openness and Action augment the practice of Compassion. The extension of appreciation and loving-kindness for all requires openness as its companion and direct application to the current situation (Action).

Horizon Practices

- The practice of Mindfulness and Surrender augments Calm. To be still, quiet, and clear requires both mindful presence and letting go.
- Practicing Relentless Intent and Compassion augment Action. Acting with relentless intent by itself can be cold, cruel, and ineffective, so it must be balanced by the appreciation and compassion that comes with knowledge of interbeing.

The Core Practice

- All practices are, of course, augmented by the Source, which gives birth to all, is in all, and is beyond all. Our Source is a radiant example of the creative energies of all eight qualities—the macrocosm that we, as microcosms, emulate.

The process is a mutual interplay. Our Source provides us with the capacity needed to embody these qualities. Then, by deliberately practicing and embodying these qualities, we develop our capacity for opening to and merging with our Source.

Part 3

The Metaphor
Warriors of Spirit

6

THE METAPHOR OF WAR

Early in the evolution of language, humans realized that saying that one thing was like another was an excellent way of defining the first thing. If I say you smell like a rose, you know what I mean (if roses have been part of your experience). Simile and metaphor are useful means for arousing images in another's consciousness in a relatively pain-free way (compared to the excruciating attention demanded by logical analysis).

Waging war (an interesting term in itself) appears to have always been a part of the experience of humankind and thus a potentially useful metaphor. In the Judeo-Christian story of the world's beginning, the two parents of humankind became aware of separateness, of an internal and external split. This duality, this splitness, opened further into the ability of Cain (an affirmed member of every human camp) to ask the question, "Am I my brother's keeper?"

The question, of course, is a statement: "I am not my brother's keeper." At that point, both my brother and I become an It—separate objects upon which war can be waged. And the war begins on two fronts: the internal war of I against me; the outer war of me against him and us against them.

War has become the human condition. We wage war to find peace—whether it is the peace of enjoying the spoils, the peace of exhaustion, the peace of sudden release from carnage, the peace of relaxed vigilance, the joyous peace of victory, the peace of balanced scales of revenge, or the peace of freedom from fear. (All these "peaces" are of course temporary and illusions.) We have no peace so we fight to attain peace. Odd, but then we are odd beings.

What is my point here? All humans are acquainted with war—thus war is a useful metaphor for the inner struggle of humans. Writing and speaking in war language creates vivid imagery in the consciousness of the reader and listener. Humans can attend to and gather meaning from the images of war. It is a place to start when we describe the journey toward and with God.

7

THE MONK-WARRIOR METAPHOR

A metaphor, to be useful, must be rich in its descriptors and predictors of action, in its ability to illuminate a course of action not previously understood (or only understood "as through a glass darkly"). The monk-warrior metaphor contains this richness and illuminative usefulness.

What is a monk-warrior? According to *Webster's New International Dictionary of the English Language*, a monk is one who has "retired from the world and devoted himself to religion in solitude; an anchoret." I like the image induced by "anchoret." An anchor rests in the calmness of the deep or is firmly affixed to solid ground. The calm of deep anchoring is the practice of the monk.

A warrior, according to the same dictionary, is one who is "engaged or experienced in war," which is "the state or fact of exerting violence against another." The concept of a nonviolent warrior evades the dictionary and *ipso facto* the general public. The definition of warrior that I choose is that of frontline responder; one who engages deeply in whatever action is called for at the moment, basing all action on the premise of no harm. "I will do no harm to you and I will not allow you to do harm to me."

A monk engages God; a warrior engages individuals. The monk-warrior does both. The monk knows that wherever she goes, she is always meeting God. The warrior knows that wherever he goes, he is always meeting himself. Together they engage God "outside the camp," in the midst of the profane.

The monk-warrior stands in the nondual and listens to the voice of the nondual. She groans with creation in the continuous birthing of God; he laughs with delight in life's delicate unfolding. The monk-warrior stands in the fires of the nondual (the primary world) and cannot be burned with dualistic fire (the divisions, pressures, and controversies of the secondary world).

The energies of the nondual radiate through the monk-warrior into the dual, engaging the world of human fabrication. The monk-warrior stands in dualism, facing and dealing with all that arises. In this arena of action, the monk-warrior follows the tactics, strategies, and battle plan provided by the nondual, listening to the wisdom of the primary world.

A monk-warrior faces and deals honestly, directly, effectively with all that arises in the dualistic world, while grounding, deepening and opening in the nondual. The monk-warrior stands in the nondual while engaging the dual. Engaged action occurs *from* the realm of non-duality *within* the realm of duality.

8

Monk and Warrior Paths as One

In the Bhagavad Gita, the warrior Arjuna raises the question as to which is the better path: the path of renunciation or the path of holy work. Should we withdraw from the secondary world or should we work within it? Krishna answers by addressing what it is that actually needs to be renounced: not work but the mental split that comes from living in the secondary world. The two paths are not separate paths. They occur simultaneously. Krishna affirms that the two paths lead to the same destination and though they appear different, they are truly one. Together, they are a formidable agent of change.

The path of holy work—engaging in action, in relationship—can be considered as the path of the warrior. The path that renounces duality—opening to and living in unity—is the path of the monk. The warrior is the arrow, and the monk is the bow that lets the arrow fly. Each is relatively useless without the other. In essence they are the same, a single functioning unit: bow-and-arrow. (Living in unity produces right relationship.)

I am aware of at least two categories of monk-warriors: those who hone their skills on the social front and those who sharpen their skills in the martial arts. Individuals in both categories open to the infinite while living in the world of flesh and bone. They deepen and ground in the nondual while engaging the "ten thousand things."

Morihei Ueshiba is an example of a warrior of hand-to-hand combat who refined the martial arts from acts of destruction to acts of creative relationship. Ueshiba took this refinement to its utmost by attempting to embody the principle of "no harm to you, no harm to me" in the martial art called Aikido (translated as "the way [*do*] of moving in harmony [*ai*] with the ultimate energy [*ki*] or nature of things"). Osensei Ueshiba developed a form of hand-to-hand combat based on relational harmony.

The monk-warriors who focus more on the social front have been called social mystics. A social mystic can be understood as someone who engages the world while embodying a consciousness of "direct intuitive observation." This is someone who lives with great presence in the realm of duality while simultaneously opening to the web of being, the interrelationship of all things. The social mystic is a living practice of being "in the world, but not of the world."

The social mystic directly engages the realm of the dual. Jesus, an exemplar of the social mystic, has often been cast as a rebel. As John Dear puts it, Jesus was "trouble from day one." This is the hallmark of a warrior: refusing to be cowed and continuing to engage no matter the size or power of the "opposing" forces.

This was true of Moses and the power of Egypt: it was true of Buddha and the forces of Mara; of Gandhi and the British Empire; of Rosa Parks and the civil authorities; of Martin Luther King and segregationist hatred; of Daniel Berrigan and Thich Nhat Hanh facing the military-industrial complex; and of Dorothy Day and socioeconomic injustice. It continues to be true for as many as dare.

Social mystics are familiar with the realm of the nondual. They have been "seized" by the nondual, and they embody more than "normal" consciousness. Through practicing stillness and listening, they continue to experience a deepening of relationship with the Source. Living within the solid ground of existence, social mystics have a deep and open knowing of reality as interbeing, as intersubjectivity, as completely relational. This realm of relational action is the place for direct application of warrior virtues.

9

Self as Mercenary

A mercenary is paid money to engage in the activity of seizing resources from others. A mercenary is a warrior of "the world." By "world" I mean all that has arisen from human thought that separates humans from the "rest" of existence.

The "world" is what the currently dominating socioeconomic system says is so: that only humans (and some humans more than others) matter; that everything other than the human consensus of reality (whatever it is we humans agree to) is a mere backdrop to the human melodrama; that everything defined as non-human (which includes some humans) is a marketable resource to be *used*.

According to this view, the Earth is to be *used*, the beings we label as "animals" are to be *used*, and the "space" and "matter" of the universe are to be *used*. Everything nonhuman is branded as a *resource* to be sacrificed to the survival and comfort of humans (or at least certain humans). Even humans are now branded as a *resource*: what was once called the Personnel Department is now Human *Resources*.

This worldview is an illusion based on the false premise that each human is separate from all else. Under the sway of this illusion, we humans, like lemmings wearing virtual-reality headpieces, march blindly toward the cliff of extinction, watching our favorite movies as we go. Here are the titles of a few of these movies:

All is Well, Technology is Savior
Gimme More Stuff
I Got Mine, You Get Yours
This World is Not My Home, I'm Just Passing Through
The Earth is a Disposable Diaper, Cause Jesus is Coming Soon
Don't Bother Me, I Got Enough Worries
and that perennial favorite: *HUH? WHUT?*

According to this worldview, the major responsibility of humans is to consume. Earth is one big Slurpee, and we are here to slurp it.

10

THE SACRED AND THE PROFANE

We humans appear to always be in a fix—in two senses of the phrase. First, we are perpetually caught in a tight place with no clear way out. Second, we are always fixing some aspect of life, always working on it. Both fixes are associated with a dualistic split. We are divided from ourselves, both intra- and inter-personally, within and without.

Being religious/spiritual folk, we regard one aspect of our being as sacred, a second aspect as profane (which originally meant "outside the temple"). We are forever working to get the profane inside the temple, while simultaneously resisting the sacred. At the same time, we work to live in accord with the sacred, while resisting the profane.

In our better moments, we rest within the sacred, while engaging the profane with loving compassion. This is the work of the bodhisattva, who has vowed to remain outside the temple, outside the camp, as long as there is one other who has not made it in. All the profane (those standing before the *fanum*, the temple) are invited in.

Of course, all of, including budding bodhisattvas, must continue inviting our own selves into the temple. This is known as spiritual practice. We must continue the practice of living within the temple of the sacred, while engaging our own profaneness. While doing so, we must continue to invite the whole world into the temple. We sacredly engage the profane within and without, all day long, each day, each moment, with each breath.

To be and do this requires a warrior of spirit.

11

WARRIOR OF SPIRIT

A warrior of spirit does not cling to body, to intellect, or to soul. A warrior of spirit lives in accord with Spirit, the Life Force that breathes us, that brings us into being at each moment.

A warrior of spirit has a body and is not the body.
Emphasis upon the body can blind us. We wash the body, oil it, perfume it, dress it, exercise it, soak it, dye it, trim it, feed it, drain it, parade it, hide it, admire it, hate it, park it, abuse it, caress it, inflate it, reduce it. And still, for all its splendor and wonder, it is a mass of urine, poop, pus, and burbling gases on a steady journey toward decay and compost. A warrior of spirit has a body and is not the body.

A warrior of spirit has an intellect and is not the intellect.
Emphasis upon the intellect can blind us. We build belief systems and mistake them for reality. We forget they are merely beliefs—habitual states of mind. Today's beliefs are tomorrow's exhibits in the House of Curiosities. Beliefs are states of mind to be trance-ended. Beliefs, no matter how holy and fervent, can blind us. A warrior of spirit has an intellect and is not the intellect.

A warrior of spirit has a soul and is not the soul.
Emphasis upon the soul can blind us. The soul is the seat of emotion, passion, and feeling. The soul can be full of love for some and hate for others. It seethes with likes and dislikes, joy and depression, righteous and murderous anger. The soul is the seat of deep attraction and strong aversion. Even our very souls can blind us. A warrior of spirit has a soul and is not the soul.

As warriors of spirit, we live in accord with spirit, which is notorious for guiding us into the realm of unconventionality. The structural rigidity of patriarchy, pseudo-matriarchy (some forms of feminism that would replace one rigid structure with another rigid structure), or our own favorite worldview are ignored in favor of the spirit's tendency to move in creative unpredictability.

A warrior of spirit is truly that: a warrior *of* the spirit; fed by spirit, directed by spirit. A warrior of spirit, seasoned by long experience, knows and trusts the voice of spirit and will continue following spirit's lead into the unknown: off the beaten paths into the newness of creativity. In this way, fires of life are born.

Part 4

Earth Weapons

*To embody spirit is to embrace—
to own—your sensual immersion in nature.
The three earth qualities and their practices allow
immediate sensual and sensible understanding,
a rooting and grounding in direct experience.*

12

THE WEAPON OF CENTERING

Keep One-Point

Centering means "collecting to a point." Wherever we focus our attention is where we "collect." This means we have a movable center. We can practice centering ourselves in negative energies: lust, anger, jealousy, worry, guilt, anxiety, fear, greed, hatred. We can center in abstract thought. We can center on caring love, in compassion. We can center ourselves in another person. We can center in immovable stillness. We can center in the moment's ceaseless movement.

Centering is a felt phenomenon. Have you ever walked a railroad track? Or a balance beam, a fallen log, or the top of a concrete wall? Recall the experience. What you were doing was centering. We feel and act one way when we are balancing (safe, serene, breath flowing easily, no thoughts, no worry) and another way when we become unbalanced (held breath, tightened muscles, flailing arms, visions of doom, alarm, and insecurity).

Centering is associated with attention. If you let your awareness rest comfortably at your balance point, you remain centered and balanced. If your attention goes elsewhere (thoughts of falling or daydreaming distraction), you become uncentered—off-balance. Centering is grounding, condensing, and deepening.

Centering is a fluid, dynamic process. We do does not *become* centered once and forever. We *practice* centering. "Experts" are those who constantly practice: centering in the morning and centering in the evening; centering at suppertime and while sleeping; centering while working, driving, and walking; centering while talking. Warriors of spirit are always centering. They perform a definable action, a clear-cut maneuver.

The warrior of spirit can, through awareness and attention, collect to *any* point of choice. Whatever is attended to becomes the warrior's center. Though there are many useful and valuable centers, our warrior ancestors have found one particular center that allows access to all other centers. For a warrior of spirit, inviting and allowing attention to settle to this vital spot is essential. This place of centering is called by different names: center of balance, one-point, and balance point. All refer to the place just below your navel and deep inside your belly.

To achieve this, collect your sense of yourself to that spot, deep within you and just below your navel. You can do this via breathing, perhaps even by envisioning and sensing the submolecular dimensions of this point. Allowing attention to settle to this vital spot is useful for detrancing yourself from the dual world. It will open you to the current of reality.

Finding Center

All humans are members of one tribe. You can tell we are because we all wear the same mark. We are the Navel Tribe, plucked from the same vine.

A first step in finding your one-point is to find your plucked place: your navel. Then put the palm of your hand on the spot just below the navel. The place beneath your hand contains the one-point. This place is also your physical center of balance.

For a moment keep your hand glued to this place. Take your other hand, lightly grasp the "glued" hand, and pull outward from there. This place you feel being pulled is your center of balance. This is the location of your internal gyroscope. It's your center of balance, your one-point.

(If you are in a wheel or motorized chair, your physical center of balance may be in another location, possibly higher up in your body or down in the chair itself. Take a moment and sense its location. See if you can sense moving from there.)

Small Bowl of Water

Another way to practice moving from your center is through the use of your imagination. Visualize a small bowl of water at your one-point location. The bowl can be as simple or ornate as you wish (mine is a small wooden bowl filled with clear, cool spring water). You may wish to get sloshing out of your system by deliberately walking in a way that sloshes the water out of your bowl. Do this in a spirit of fun and laughter.

When done sloshing, settle for a while. Make sure your bowl is refilled. Now walk around without disturbing the still surface of the water. A common tendency is to walk stiffly while holding one's breath (for fear of spilling the water). Instead, walk with ease, with relaxed arms and legs. Breathe deeply and slowly and smoothly.

The Head: One-Point Comparison

This exercise is designed to allow you a direct experience of the difference between moving from the one-point and moving from the head. The head is chosen as a comparison point because most of us are accustomed to living in our heads. We move around preoccupied with internal chatter (sometimes called "rooftop" chatter).

Place the palm of one hand on your forehead. Imagine that it is stuck there. Begin walking by grasping the stuck hand with your other hand and pulling. Continue to pull yourself along. Sense how it feels to move when your attention is focused within your head. (I've noticed that many people on my university campus walk from their heads. Some of them even walk with their heads preceding the rest of their body.)

Now place your hand just below your navel and pull from there with the other hand. Walk from this place of one-point for a while. Sense how it feels.

Switch back and forth—walking from the head, then walking from the one-point—until you can vividly sense the difference in balance, in mood, and in awareness. Say the differences aloud or write them down so that the intellect, as well as the body, can comprehend.

Mindfulness of One-Point in Daily Life

In the beginnings of practice, one-point is maintained, like any other skill, only through conscious awareness. Moving, living, and opening from one-point will eventually, however, become as familiar as breathing: no thinking required. A way to practice maintaining one-point is to consciously go to there as soon as wake up. Get out of bed from the one-point; let the one-point take you to your morning rituals; move from the one-point through the day. Drive from the one-point. Eat from the one-point. Talk from the one-point. Listen from the one-point. Write or use your keyboard from the one-point. Walk from the one-point. Sit down and get up from the one-point.

One-Point Walking

Observe a child learning to walk. The child gets up, falls down, gets up, falls down, over and over and over. The child is like a small samurai embodying the warrior admonition: "Seven times down, eight times up!"

As my son Phil has pointed out to me, walking is the art of controlled falling. This controlled falling is learned so well that our continuous balancing is largely out of awareness. Balancing is a process that never stops, a process that eventually occurs at infinitesimal levels.

Meditation and medium come from the same ancient root words that had to do with measuring, finding the middle point. Meditation can be defined as a continuous aligning with the middle, an inner balancing. Walking can be consciously meditational. It can be moving meditation.

Connecting Heart and One-Point

To develop an even stronger sense of the one-point, you may wish to practice breathing into your heart and then down to the one-point. Stand with weight equally distributed on both feet, which are about shoulder width apart and flat on the floor or ground. Visualize, sense, and feel the crown of your head as suspending from a heavenly cord. Breathe in to your heart area. When breathing out, breathe down to the one-point.

The heart begins to receive more energy, to be bathed in energy, to energize. The one-point becomes firmer, calmer, more dynamically still. Instead of living only in your head, you are practicing residing in the one-point and in the heart. You are beginning the practice of going out of your mind and into the Mind.

Grounding Exercise

Settle. Relax. Breathe. Allow the upper body to be suspended from a heavenly cord attached to the crown of your head. Turn your awareness to the balance points on the soles of your feet. Visualize roots growing out of these points into the ground. Let your awareness move to the submolecular level by sensing the root tips as one-cell thick, so small they can move into the tiniest crevices of the earth. Sense the root tips gently moving into and through these crevices. Allow your roots to grow.

Midline Power

The midline of the body is the place that projects the greatest power and energy. This line proceeds from the mid-sagittal suture at the crown of the head downward through the body, a razor-thin line between the right and left sides of the body. You project energy outward from this line. When focusing (on anything!), align this area with the exact center of the point of focus. (For example, if sitting at a computer keyboard, align the midline of the body with the keyboard, directly facing it. This allows balanced responsive movement with the entire keyboard.)

When you are ready, allow your midline awareness to extend beyond the head to the limitless sky (the sky becomes your head) and through the Earth so that you are rooted and grounded. If you wish, allow the midline to extend through the Earth and out into the sky on the other side of the sphere.

Your midline then goes from sky to sky while firmly anchored in the Earth.

Allow awareness to return again and again throughout the day to your midline (from head to ground). This can produce an exquisite sense of balance.

Stance and Midline: The Earthly Triangle

You may often find yourself standing with your feet together, as if your ankles are tied together with a rope. This makes you a pushover. A more balanced way of standing is with the feet about shoulder width apart, toes pointing forward, knees slightly bent.

Allow your midline to be poised between Heaven and Earth as described above. Allow awareness to settle at the soles of your feet. Subtly shift your weight toward the toes. Notice the sensation of balance/imbalance as you do so. Allow your weight to slowly shift to the heels. Notice when you have shifted too far back.

Continue this slow movement back and forth until you sense the center point, the center of balance for each foot. Visualize this balance point as a small circular spot on the sole of each foot. When connected by an imaginary horizontal line, these spheres of balance form the bottom line of your Earthly Triangle.

Become increasingly aware of your one-point, the balance point about two inches below your navel, which is the apex of the triangle. Open to an awareness of the connection of the one-point with the balance point on the sole of the left foot and on the sole of the right foot. Sense the existence of your Earthly Triangle: an isosceles triangle with the one-point at its peak. Visualize internal energy moving up, down, across, and around the triangle.

Your Centering Practice

For this manual to be of any practical use to you, it is essential that you find and adopt centering practices that are most natural and suited to you. Perhaps it is imaging the small bowl of water at your core as you move through the day, or one of the other practices described above. Perhaps it is none of those.

Take a few moments and open to understanding what you do naturally that allows you to settle and center. Or, if you do not already have a centering practice, which of the above practices or variation of one of these practices might you embody in your daily life? Choose only one at this time.

Then write it down somewhere you can refer to it often: *My centering practice in daily life is...*

13

THE WEAPON OF MINDFULNESS

Attention! Attention! Attention!

To be any place other than *here* can be an invitation to a rude awakening. Mindfulness is the practice of fully living in this ever-changing present moment. When our awareness goes away (to dreams of the past or future or to a world of fantasy), we lose momentum. Mindful presence allows energetic being.

Mindfulness cuts through illusion, including the illusion of a separate self, which is the pervasive sickness of our society. Mindfulness is sharp, discerning; it takes no prisoners. Mindfulness stands naked in the universe with no protective clothing. It is the true occupation of a bodhisattva, an awakening warrior of radiant origin.

Do you *mind*? When we ask this question of another, we sometimes mean, "You are in my way. Don't you care? Will you readjust your position to allow me to continue on my way?" Another shade of meaning points to attention and awareness (or lack of awareness). If truly we "mind," then we are aware and attentive. The question can also imply, "Where is your mind? Is your mind somewhere else?" The question thus refers to the degree of presence or absence.

Minding then means to care, to be aware, to be attentive, to be present, and to shift and change according to current reality.

The practice of mindfulness, the cultivation of nonjudgmental moment-to-moment awareness, includes:

- *Attentional training*: Practicing the ability to place our attention where we choose and to remove our attention when we choose.
- *Being nonjudgmental toward self and others*: This does not mean that you don't know the difference between acceptable and unacceptable behavior. It means that you don't make an idol out of whomever

or whatever you are being judgmental toward. "Idol" means your eye is dull; your eye becomes stuck there at the judgment point and cannot see further. Since whatever you attend to you become, you become that stuckness.

- *Being present*: Everything that is going on is going on right here, right now. Now is the time. It is always already *now*. When we are not here now, we are not at the place of action. We are not being frontline responders. And that is always a personal choice. We are masters at zoning out.

- *Being aware*: Images that come with sensations, feelings, and thoughts carry us away. Part of mindfulness practice is recognizing when we are zoning out, away from *now*; recognizing our own state of consciousness, its furnishings, and perhaps deciding to rearrange the furniture. "I don't like that old sad sofa, that rigid straight chair, that bed of nails, that dartboard with the picture of the person I love most to hate." Or maybe you decide to keep those furnishings. That is, of course, up to you. The point is to become aware of the habitual furnishings of your mind.

Deadly States of Mind

Martial arts teachers use many "minding" terms when they write about their art and when they train students: right mindedness, no-mind, mind like the moon, mind like water, immovable mind, no-abiding mind, original mind, placement of the mind, mind-stopping, and so on. In the martial arts, the state of a person's mind is considered as highly important.

Our attitude is manifested mentally, spiritually, and physically. It is clearly visible. The "wrong" attitude can open us to serious injury or death. In martial arts (and in daily life), there are at least four ways of mind that can be deadly: the full mind, the stopped mind, the led mind, and ordinary mind.

The Full Mind

He checked his mind from time to time. When looking within, he found that much of the time he was full. When thoughts and images occupied his mind, when emotions flooded his heart, he had no time, no room for anything or anyone. When his mind was full, he went through the day as if blind and deaf, insensitive to all but mind-chatter and emotional surges. He became a victim of fullness. There was no room for anyone but himself.

Once there was a young Japanese swordsman full of pride and self-importance. He used every opportunity to show off his skill with the sword, even challenging and killing those who were obviously no match for him. One day, full to overflowing with his swaggering ego, he confronted Miyamoto Musashi (who later authored *Gorin No Sho, The Book of Five Rings*). Musashi declined the invitation to an immediate duel. An agreement was reached to meet on a river island at dawn the next day.

Before dawn, the young man strutted before the onlookers, proclaiming what he was going to do to Musashi—*if* that coward ever showed up! Meanwhile, Musashi asked a boatman to row him to the island of encounter. On the way, he whittled a rough sword out of an extra wooden oar.

In a relaxed yet focused state of mind, Musashi stepped out of the boat, walked directly to the awaiting braggart, and struck one blow on the crown of the man's skull. The man with the mind full of himself fell dead.

The young man obviously had the wrong state of mind. He was saturated with egotistical pride. Musashi, on the other hand, had a "free and open mind."

The Stopped Mind

When someone asked Willard Lindstrom, an accomplished South Dakota guitarist, piano player, and beekeeper, his secret to making music, Willard said simply, "Don't stop."

A second type of mind that leads to defeat is the stopped mind. A stopped mind produces an opening. The enemy appears and slashes through the opening.

When your mind (awareness) stops, you stop. Like a fly in the web of a spider, you are caught in doubt, tangled in hesitation, paralyzed by indecision. One step toward unfreezing yourself is to realize that you are all three (fly, web, and spider). Then you can begin laughing at your amazing ability to trance yourself into stuckness.

Deliberate stopping of the mind, called a *suki* in Japanese, is one of the weapons used by martial artists. In stopping the other's mind (often by a devastating shout), the attacker has the other at his mercy.

The truth of this can also be seen when you have a conversation with someone where each of you are attempting to sway the other to a particular point of view. As long as you keep a verbal and nonverbal flow with immediate and relevant responses, you cannot be "pinned down." If you falter and hesitate, however, the other person picks up the beat.

In daily life, a stopped mind is one that is caught in fantasy, in doubt, in any internal state that decreases or eliminates awareness. A stopped mind is a dead mind. The person is a victim of stupor-idity.

The Led Mind

Do you remember the childhood trick of pointing to a person's chest and asking, "What's that?" as if something inappropriate (a bug, spilled food) is there? If the person falls for it and look down, your pointing finger quickly becomes a tool for flipping him under the nose or chin. You have led his mind, and he has paid the consequences.

The mind that is led is an attached mind: attached to some aspect of internal or external circumstances. The mind sticks like glue to a feinting movement or to a sword blade—or, in daily life, to a pre-established plan or a rigid belief. As a result, the attached mind does not reflect current reality.

A swordsman named Hidetsuna, who lived in fifteenth-century Japan, passed through a village where he found everyone confused and anxious. A man had taken a child hostage and barricaded himself in a barn. He was threatening to kill the child if anyone approached.

Hidetsuna put aside his swords, had his head shaved, donned a monk's robe, and approached the barn armed with only two rice balls, one in each hand. He told the alarmed (and hungry) man that he had brought food for the child and for the man.

Hidetsuna tossed one rice ball to the man, who released the child and caught it in his left hand. Hidetsuna immediately tossed the other rice ball. The man dropped his sword and caught the second rice ball. Hidetsuna stepped in and subdued him.

This man's mind was led by the tossed rice balls. As a result, his mind could not take in his current reality.

The led mind pursues a reactive path. All other paths are closed. Free, unrestrained, 360-degree awareness is not a possibility.

Trance Mind

Most of us attend to our internal dialogue most of the time. By attending, we direct energy to it, and it grows even more powerful. We begin to identify with our thoughts. We believe we are the internal dialogue. This is a form of insanity: the inability to shift one's attention, a stuckness.

We entrance ourselves. Like master hypnotists, we give ourselves repetitive suggestions. We convince ourselves that we are *this* way, the world is *that* way, and the future is like *this* or *that*. We repeat these hypnotic commands to ourselves and dare anyone to deny that our hypnotic suggestions are anything but reality. We repeat scenarios of doom as if fingering a demonic rosary.

"Monday" is a trance state. So is "Friday." Dogs don't know it's Monday (except by our trance behavior). Neither do the trees, small children, flowers, the sun, the earth. You are the one who decides that since this particular appearance of the sun is named "Monday," you will imbue it with Monday-like qualities. You are the one who decides. Oh sure, you may have committed to certain activities. But you don't have to let it be "Moan Day."

Trance Dance

If you are going to be in a trance, don't do it half-heartedly. Really get into it! Trance yourself on purpose and with full awareness. For example, if one of your favorite trances is worry, take your usual worries and fashion them into a worry mantra, a litany of worries, complaints, and fears. Write them down. Capsulate them, make them into one or two sentences or a few phrases. It's helpful if it's rhythmic. At the end of your worry mantra, add a phrase (repeated twice) invoking the aid of the powers of the universe, such as "Help me O God, Help me O God" or "Help! Help!" Every time you feel like worrying, recite it like a Gregorian chant. (Caution: Do not use self-limiting phrases like "I can't" as in "I can't pay these bills. I can't pay these bills. Help! Help!" Instead, take the "I" out of it as in "Bills are unpaid. Bills are unpaid. Help! Help!")

Why-ning and How-ling.

Why-ning is a part of ordinary mind. Why-ning refers to the tendency to ask, "Why? Why me? Why must I do this? Why am I like I am? Why is the world this way? Why, why, why, why, why?" This is why-ning.

Why? Pick your answer: genetics, environment, karma, family, job, society, early childhood experiences, Adam and Eve and the serpent, television, other people, God, the Devil, the Big Bang, the Great Unfolding . . . The list goes on and on.

Focusing on "why?" leaves little space to create personal change. I can stay on my therapeutic couch of analysis forever.

A little understanding of why is okay, but a more important question is "how?" After I know what I want to change, I need to know how. How? By doing this and not doing that. By being this and not being that. By attending to this and not attending to that.

Stop why-ning. Start how-ling.

Stance Affects Trance

"Stand up straight," my grandmother often told me. She was wiser than I knew at the time. Following her advice affected far more than the physical body. Physical stance is an ally in clear seeing.

Many of us are entranced much of the time. Even though our bodies are here, our minds travel to other places and times: reliving conversations with others, envisioning next steps in daily activities. These travelings in past, present, future, and hyperspace are trance states.

For example, I may trance myself into believing that I am "George Breed," a social phenomenon composed of other's perceptions and expectations. If I'm not careful, I might live out a portion of life doing my best to either conform to or react against these perceptions and expectations. I would rather see clearly and not be entranced.

The way we stand and sit affects the subtle energies of our consciousness. To experience this, sit with your elbows resting on your knees and head in your hands and look down. Become aware of the mood tone of this posture.

Now relax, breathe, and shake your hands as if flinging water droplets from your fingers. This allows releasing of mood.

Next, sit erect in a chair, both feet flat on the floor. Visualize a golden or silver heavenly cord from which you are suspended. The cord is attached to the crown of your head and extends upward into infinity. While grounded by the chair and floor, your upper body is suspended by the heavenly cord. Let breathing flow. Become aware of your mood. Notice the differences between your mood tone in this posture and the mood tone in the first posture.

Persons often report that the second posture is "easier" and "more relaxing." With awareness, you may find that you put yourself into postures (like the first posture) that produce trance states of negativity. It pays to park your body in a posture that generates positive energy. No one is in charge of this but you.

Chiltan Posture

One Flagstaff winter morning I opened to the Chiltan posture. My dogs and I were moving through the ponderosa pine forest before sunrise, the just-past-full moon grinning from the west on the new snow, while the morning star blazed gloriously in the eastern sky. The north-pointing finger of the Big Dipper singled out the San Francisco Peaks, capped with snow and framed in a break in the pines. The near peak, Agassiz, looked like Mount Fuji in the moonlight.

I stood facing the morning star, feet shoulder width apart, left hand on one-point, right hand on heart. My right hand energized, warmed, and strengthened the heart; the left hand opened the one-point. After the heart and one-point were vibrating warmly in the cold pre-dawn air, I switched hands. I found that the right hand on the one-point and the left hand on the heart connected one-point and heart.

I turned to the west and opened to the spirit of the moon in the same way: first, right hand on heart, left hand on one-point, and then switching hands.

I turned to the south and faced two oaks, standing side by side, each with gracefully extended snow-covered arms glistening in the moonlight. My left hand was on my heart, my right on the one-point. The energy of the one-point, activated earlier, moved through my right palm, into the right arm, up and across the shoulders, and through the left arm into the heart chakra. The energy reversed itself and spiraled from the heart into the one-point. The energy then moved straight up and down connecting the heart and one-point in one shimmering vibration.

After a while, I moved through the forest and found myself standing and experiencing the blessing of a large snow-draped oak. I opened to its Chiltan spirit. Joy moved through me. I turned and saw the moon hanging over four distinctly individual ponderosa pines. The vision of each was touched by the faint rosy hue of the soon-to-appear sun. Moonlight still fell on the snow. I looked at the oak. Something almost imperceptible moved in its upper middle branches, something at its heart. I laughed with pleasure and moved on through the snow.

Going Out of Your Mind

The man was highly intellectual. He sat in my office caught in the web of intellect. While he continued to speak, I wrote a note on a small card and handed it to him. He read it aloud, "Go out of your mind." He looked confused, then serious. He burst out laughing.

In our culture, the phrase "out of your mind" means crazy, irresponsible. "Are you out of your mind?" is a question asked of someone behaving in a bizarre or unexpected fashion. We value total identification with the mind or intellect. We still put Descartes ("I think, therefore I am") before the "horse" (our vehicles: the physical body and the awareness body of infinite extension).

Once, when I was asked to talk to a university career women's group, I looked up "career" in my mammoth 1918 Webster's dictionary. Career, I discovered, has its roots in a word that means "to gallop swiftly on a track like a running horse." The word "careen" (to veer almost out of control) is a close cousin.

Many of us have multiple careers and are galloping swiftly through the day. It behooves us to pay attention to our horse during all this. If we go out of our mind and allow the full experience of embodying, we find that our horse has wisdom of its own. Going out of our mind allows attuning to the wisdom of the physical body, which opens further into the awareness body (you extend much further than you *think*).

The warrior often has no time to think. When someone comes swinging, the "horse" is already moving. The same is true in everyday life. In driving a car, you may have had the experience of braking or swerving quickly, with no thought. The horse takes over. The horse has great wisdom.

In going out of the mind, we open to relationship. In relationship, separation does not exist. We don't act; in other words, a "subject" does not "do something" to an "object"). Action *is*. What occurs is called forth from what is. Whatever comes to pass is called for by the flow of the situation. Future action unfolds out of current process. The Tao taos the Tao. The Flow flows the Flow. The Wave waves the Wave.

In the martial arts, this phenomenon is known as the sword that swings itself. The swordsperson has no thought of harming another, no thought of revenge or of dispensing justice, no thought of self-protection. The swordsperson is simply (and vividly) present. The attacker calls the sword into action.

When the sword swings itself, the ego is not involved. When the ego (sense of separate self) swings the sword, the ego is responsible for whatever happens (usually a bloody mess). When the sword of spirit swings, no ego is in sight. Right action occurs. The action provides what is called for, no more, no less.

Presence

A bear of a man sat in my office. He was moving through troubled times at home and at work. The man chuckled. "Well the way I figure it, if you can't do anything else, you can still suit up and show up. Isn't that right?" I could only laugh with him and agree.

The man's "suit" consisted of presence: troubled but *here*, hurting but *here*. He was determined to continue to face and deal. No strategies, no weapons, no plans other than to "suit up" and "show up." No running, no hiding, simply present.

Life has its own rhythm. At times it is easy to maintain open awareness. At other times, it feels almost impossible. We seem to open and close like some exotic blooming flower, opening and closing to a rhythm we do not understand.

When we can't see clearly and we feel "shut in" and our vision obscured, an effective response is to allow. Allow, even give blessings to, the current state of awareness and it will be given room to change. Transformation occurs.

If nothing else, be simply present.

Vanquishing Negative Thought

You can take steps to rid yourself of negative and judgmental thoughts. First, before you throw the thought away, see if it contains any useful information. Do not throw a repetitive thought away until you see if it has something to say to you.

As an example, if the thought comes into my mind: "I talk too much," I want to take a look at that. I want to observe the full extent of my talkativeness. Am I indeed flooding the air with my words?

After extracting any useful information, the next step is *pffft!* a method taught by Aikido Sensei Koichi Tohei. Find an index finger. Place it to your lips. Vigorously utter the sound *pffft!* and throw the thought with your index finger to the far horizon, to outer infinity. Body and mind acting together are more powerful than either alone. You combine the bodily gesture of throwing it away with the imagery of that thought being flung to the far corners of the universe.

A participant from the Navaho Nation recently told our mindfulness group that the Navaho way is to say *pah!* I like that. It has a gentler sense of release. *Pah!*

Whether you *pffft!* or *pah!* do not stand there looking for the thought to come back. Immediately turn your attention to something else: a predetermined thought, an affirmation of some kind, a prayer. Or turn your attention to whatever you are doing. If you are ironing your clothes, turn your attention to ironing your clothes. If you are driving, turn your attention to driving.

If the negative thought arises again, as soon as you are aware of it, throw it away again with a gesture and sound, and then turn your attention immediately to another place. Since attention directs energy, if you pay attention to this negative thought after extracting its useful information, then you are giving it more power. You are allowing it to stay in your mind and it becomes more and more powerful. To allow it to dissolve, you must turn your attention to something else.

Attention directs energy. What is attended to becomes energized (more powerful). What is not attended to becomes de-energized and eventually fades into oblivion.

Formal and Informal Practice

Mindful awareness can be practiced both formally and informally. Formal practice means to have a certain time and location for sitting quietly, to honor a specific *form*. This could mean parking your body so it doesn't fall over, sitting in a dignified posture, eliminating external distraction, creating a sacred space, and so on. Informal practice, on the other hand, uses daily life with all its unexpectancies, distractions, interactions, and routines as an arena for mindfulness.

Formal practice provides a base, a ground for informal practice. Daily life practice ensures that mindfulness is part of your being and isn't an aspect that can only thrive in a "hothouse" environment.

Your Mindfulness Practice

Consider creating (or deepening) a *formal* mindfulness practice for you. What time of day might it occur? Early morning? Noon? Evening? Where might you sit? In what chair? On what cushion? Can you turn your phone off during this time? Do you need to notify other family members so they can support your practice?

For *daily life* practice of mindfulness, consider using a centering exercise (for example, the imaginary small bowl of water) as you move through the day—or periodically attend to your breath to call yourself into the *now*. Practice being actively present in whatever you are currently doing (driving, talking, listening, walking, performing a task).

Make notes about your mindfulness practice. Refer to them often. *How will you embody mindfulness in your life?*

14

THE WEAPON OF RELENTLESS INTENT

Seven times down, eight times up!

Energy practice (*kung fu*) means deliberately embodying unremitting attention, continuously lending energy to a single pursuit. Energy practice is calm and steady. It is the practice of relaxed relentlessness.

Embodying relentless intent is like praying without ceasing: a constant connection with the universe. In Aikido terms, it is extending positive energy in all directions. Relentless intent means total involvement, while simultaneously letting go. It means acting from the depths of our being with no clinging.

Isshinryu (the name of the karate discipline I first learned) means "to throw oneself wholly into the action without any other thought at all." Hokusai has an energetic drawing of a warrior on horseback leaping from a cliff into a roaring mountain stream. The warrior and the horse are as one. The warrior is still and relaxed while the horse is moving with vibrant openness. Total commitment, nothing held in reserve. With such a state of being, the mission has already been accomplished while it is being accomplished.

A Native American woman I know spoke with some of us about the custom of men of the tribe during hunting season. When the family or community needs meat, the hunters condense their focus, withdrawing from verbal and sensual contact with their mates and others. They concentrate deeply on the specific animal they invite to give its life. A relationship is formed. By the time the hunter physically leaves for the hunt, the animal's sacrifice is a done deal. The mission is accomplished before it is accomplished.

Relentless Intent and Co-Creation

God has been defined as a circle with no circumference whose center is everywhere. You are one of those centers where universal creation abides. Without our relentless intent, the wellspring of creativity is clogged with the debris of our fragmentation. When we keep willing it, it will be done. We are co-creators with the universe.

To some extent, we will to be the way we are. Personality concretions (sometimes called disorders)—being "set" in our ways—are partly due to choices we made and continue to make in our lives. Personality concretions arise from closure due to fear, anger, or confusion (or all three). We have relentless intent to stay in the shape we are in. ("I am the way I have defined myself to be, and don't tell me any different. My mind is made up like a bed in the morning, and I don't want any strange ideas trying to slide beneath my covers.") We limit ourselves through relentless story telling: I am *this* way. The world is *that* way. I must always be *this* way. The world must always be the way I perceive it to be.

Without relentless intent to tell a different story, we will remain confined in our mental cubicles. With only vaporous intent, we will use any perceived obstacle as justification for remaining in our prison. We may rebel but we will not revolt. Without relentless intent, we will yield to the pressures of others who have strong interest in our remaining the same. We will follow the will of humans rather than the will of spirit and co-creation with the universe.

With relentless intent, we ruthlessly vanquish all inner obstacles to openness and presence. With relentless intent, we do not cling to *any* element of secondary reality. With relentless intent, we continue opening to primary reality. We are truly warriors of spirit: of the primary Life Force. We know no bounds.

Mind and Body as One

When our mind and body are moving in the same direction, we are strong. If the mind is thinking of something separately from what the body is doing, we lose strength. As Jesus says in the Gospel of Thomas, "When the two become one, we can say to the mountain to move and it will move." People demonstrate this to themselves quite readily in my workshops.

I invite folk to think of something they truly want; it doesn't matter what it is as long as they have a strong urge to attain it. The group moves to the other side of the room from me. Each person walks toward me twice: once with the desired something behind them so that they are walking away from it; once with it ahead of them so they are walking toward it. I extend my arm horizontally so that I catch each person across the chest at shoulder level. They cannot be stopped when their mind and body are moving as one.

Hauling the Meat: Just Take the One More Next Step

All of have days of relative lifelessness and fatigue, with no internal music and no external rhythm. On those days, all we can do is "haul the meat." Hauling the meat means to keep putting one step in front of another, to allow one breath to follow another. Even with no music or rhythm, maintain movement. Eventually, rhythm and music will appear. [Caution: two or more meat-hauling days in a row are a sign that something in your life needs contemplative attention.]

Diamond Sharp

A diamond in its clarity and brilliance cuts right through. No effort. The very nature of its being allows slicing through. Relentless intent is diamond like. With relentless intent no obstacles appear. Everything is in the Way, so no thing is in the way.

Diamond sharp does not mean harsh engaging. Diamond sharp intent responds appropriately with each moment's circumstances. Diamond sharp can be very soft and quiet. Diamond sharp means appropriate engaging.

For example, gentle laughter often cuts right through imagined obstacles. This does not mean that gentle laughter is used as a deliberate ploy. Appropriate responses arise concurrently with imagined obstacles (person, thought, and situation). Such responses include gentle laughter, calm silence, or even a sudden shout! Diamond sharp refers to the deep intent. The manifestation of diamond sharp may take many forms.

The Silver Cord

This practice is especially useful for walking up an incline, whether mountain or stairs, though it's also wonderful when walking or running on a more level plane. While walking or running, visualize a slender strong filament, a silver cord, extending from your one-point to a winch or reel attached to a tree, boulder, or building several hundred feet in front of you. Allow yourself to be "reeled in" by this silver cord. Relax all muscles not essential to your movement. When you do so, you are moving from your one-point, from your physical center of balance.

Your Practice of Intent

The practices of *centering* and of *mindfulness* can be a strong basis for developing your *intent*. *Pure* intent comes from your mindful core or center, uncontaminated by any form of cognitive-emotional affliction (fear, anger, regret, desire, and stupor). Pure intent aligns with primary reality and may be at odds with "world" reality.

Your practice of pure intent comes along with your practice of centering and mindful presence. After settling and centering and relaxing into the Now, reflect upon your intent for this day, for this moment, for this life. In what arenas of action will your intent express itself?

Your intent is like an arrow released from your core. What are you intending for your life? What are you intending for this day? What is your intent for practicing your intent?

Part 5

Heaven Weapons

*The three Earth weapons alone are out of balance.
To be centered, mindful, and relentless is not enough.
Each has its complement in a weapon of the heavens,
and with its partner, each is to be manifested in
(horizontal) daily life action.
The three Heaven principles and practices
allow clear and infinite openness.*

15

THE WEAPON OF OPENING

Have 360-degree awareness.

Opening allows us to sense all other beings while being sensed, to live in the realm of intersubjectivity. Opening coincides with releasing or letting go (the essence of both forgiving and healing). Opening allows us to freely merge with all that is, to be at home in the universe.

Some of the persons I see as a psychotherapist are in the process of closing their hearts because they are in pain. A closed heart feels like a knot in your chest. Breathing becomes shallow. Anxiety attacks occur. Bitterness sets in. Stupor is sought. A closed heart is death.

Healing (making whole, hale, and hearty) requires an open heart. Pain can still arise but it also dissipates as we open to the rhythm of life. Openness means no clinging: no clinging to pain, no clinging to joy. (*Cling, cling, cling goes the folly.*)

Contemplation: Living in the Temple

My Webster's dictionary definition of meditation is "to keep the mind in a state of contemplation." Contemplation means to go to the *templum*, an ancient space for observation marked out by the highest class of official diviners, the augurs. Ancient Rome had a college of augurs whose sole duty was the interpretation of signs, especially through observing the flight of birds. To do so they needed a clear and open space, the *templum*.

The augurs moved to the clear and open space with expectancy (predetermined signs would answer specific questions) and with no expectancy (unexpected portents or omens could occur). With expectation and no-expectation, with mind and no-mind, they looked for one of several specific events to occur. Like scientists awaiting one of several possible sets of data to appear, while staying open to the unexpected, the augurs sat in contemplation.

(Shortly after reading about augurs, I went to the forest with my dogs. I stood in a clear open space. A red-tailed hawk—one of my totems—appeared. The hawk flew about twenty feet above my head, looking down at me, circling twice, and then shooting out of view. I stood meditancing.)

When we meditate or sit mindfully, we go to the *templum*, we prepare for insight by moving to an inner space of clarity and openness. We open in con-templ-ation, move into the temple, and become one with the universal template.

Open Awareness

I was in the grocery store the other day, picking up a few things for the home. Though the store was full of people, the only one who saw me was a three-year-old, perched in his mother's shopping cart. Our eyes met with clear awareness. No words hid us from each other. The adults were lost in thought, in self-induced trance states. The three-year-old was wide awake. We saw each other's openness. Our open presence was a blaze of awareness that extended outward in all directions.

Such presence comes with calmness, with the absence of the will of separateness, with letting go of words and thoughts, with allowing life's flow. This relaxed extension of awareness is called "extension of ki" by Aikido folk. A circle or sphere provides the perfect imagery for describing ki extension. A sphere depicts 360-degree awareness, awareness in all directions.

To provide an example from everyday life, bring to awareness the experience of driving a car. Driving a car requires 360-degree consciousness; an awareness of what is going on behind, to the left, to the right, to the immediate front, to the distant front. The driver's awareness radar perpetually scans the spherical area radiating outwards from her center.

Any movement or potential movement in that 360-degree field of consciousness receives immediate attention and relaxed response. This 360-degree awareness can be condensed or expanded at will through attention.

Galeropia: Clear and Cheerful Vision

Galeropia (gal-uh-rope-e-ah) is a word combining the Greek *galeros* (cheerful) and *opsis* (vision). A medical term, galeropia means exceptional clearness of vision. Clear vision is cheerful vision.

Cheerful vision is not smile-button, Pollyannaish, bubbleheaded vision. Cheerful vision is not accomplished with a noodle full of meringue. Cheerful vision is practical, down-to-earth and expanding-past-earth vision.

Derived from the Middle English word *chere* (face or welcome), cheer at one time meant countenance: the outward look or appearance. It eventually came to mean spirit, state of mind, or heart. The word *cher* refers to courage (French: *couer*) and heart.

"Be of good cheer," said Jesus, the Ki Master. Have courage and heart. Be of good cheer. Have a good countenance toward all. Face all with good spirit, good mind, and good heart. ("Good" originally meant fitting or belonging together, as in "and God saw that it was good." The creation of the heavens and earth was good. When creation was flung into being, God pitched a perfect fit.)

Be of cheerful and clear vision (awareness). Galerope through the day.

Settling Down

A prerequisite to open awareness is allowing yourself to relax, to settle down. Settling down is an inner experience. You can feel the muscles and the cells of your body relaxing and letting go. You're no longer "bearing up" under the stresses and demands of your current trance state. You settle into your center. You let go of all else.

Please put down anything you are doing and let your awareness move to your breathing. When you breathe in, breathe into your heart area. Visualize, sense, and feel that you are breathing into your heart. Use your childhood imagination.

After breathing into your heart, when breathing out breathe down into your one-point, just below your belly button. Breathe into your heart, and then, when breathing out, feel that breath go down to the one-point. If your breath does not go all the way down, be patient. Over time, it will.

Breathe in to heart. Breathe down to center. Allow settling down. After settling down, extend positive energy in all directions. "Positive" refers to clear sensing. Negativity blocks our field of vision. For example, fear does not allow us to see clearly.

In extending clear positive energy in all directions, you will be exquisitely aware of your surroundings. You will also be expanding your sphere of influence. In *The Method of Zen*, Eugene Herrigel writes of this expansion of the sphere of influence as spreading your field of power around you in ever-widening rings.

Settle down. Extend clear positive awareness in all directions.

Spaces Between Thoughts

As I sit quietly centering, I pay attention to thoughts going by. I see my thoughts like boats on a river, like a train with cars. I begin to pay attention to the spaces between thoughts. Sometimes it seems as if these spaces are razor's edge thin.

I continue to attend to the spaces, the intervals between thoughts. The spaces become larger and larger.

By giving attention to the spaces between thoughts, energy is directed to the spaces rather than to the thoughts themselves, and the mind gradually becomes empty, empty in a positive way. As the mind empties of preconception and thought, awareness opens to the Larger Context.

The extension of open awareness toward infinity in all directions (a spherical 360 degrees, a sphere with no bounds) becomes comfortable and natural.

Condensing and Expanding

Park your body in an alert yet relaxed and stable posture. Breathe in deeply, smoothly, calmly. Breathe out beyond the far horizon. Visualize a sphere of energy the size of an orange at your center of balance, about two inches below your navel and deep inside. Halve it in size. Halve it again. Continue to halve it until you reach subatomic realms and the Infinity of Inside.

Then double it and continue doubling until you and the Earth are enveloped in a light-filled sphere of energy. Continue to expand until you reach galactic realms and the Infinity of Outside.

Condense again. Repeat the process for as long as is comfortable.

Your Openness Practice

Notice the times during the day when you feel more open and able to engage life situations. Notice the times of closure, of your energy condensing. While honoring your natural rhythm of opening and closing, consider that with a relaxed spirit you can stay open to the energy of our Source, to the wellspring from which all life flows. Maintaining openness to the Source is essential to spiritual life. This "rooting" openness allows us to remain open to daily life.

What is the quality of your openness? Do you have calm awareness—or is it agitated hypervigilance? What is your openness practice? What are your practices that allow you to remain aware?

16

THE WEAPON OF SURRENDERING

Enter and blend.

Relentless intent can be in the service of the ego—the aspect of our being that falls prey to the illusion of separateness. The coupling of relentless intent and ego allows us to see all others as objects, as fair game for aggressive manipulations that serve our own interests. Relentless intent and ego are prime ingredients of insanity. Relentless intent must be combined with surrender.

We surrender to the universe, to the great mystery that actively breathes us. Surrendering means dropping our "self" stories, no matter how entertaining and fascinating and intriguing, in favor of the larger story. We declare ourselves planetary and universal citizens.

Surrender means to drop all self-induced trances. The word surrender points toward "rend." When we surrender to the universe, we are torn apart and rendered as someone new. No longer a pleasure-seeking, pain-avoiding, alienated protoplasmic blob, we become an integral embodying of the universe itself, of the great mystery, of the origin unfolding, evolving.

To Be Rendered

On our South Dakota farmette (26 acres along the Vermillion River), we lived with an assortment of critters: hogs, sheep, chickens, ducks, and horses. When something died that was not edible (we were active carnivores), we called the Rendering Man. He would whisk the carcass away and assist its transformation into further usefulness.

To surrender means to allow oneself to be totally rendered. It is a painful process. The old carcass is whisked away, its parts put together into new, imaginative and useful ways.

A friend said over the phone as we spoke of surrender, "You mean I have to give up and accept defeat?"

"Yes," I said. "Give *up*. Accept *the feet*. Do both at the same time. It's called embodying heaven and earth."

Total Abandon

A Ronin is a warrior with no earthly master, no organized clan; a warrior who roams outside the established camps. He allows no part of the human consensus world to dominate. He follows the spirit of the Life Force.

Becoming and being a Ronin is an essential stage in the life of Spirit. At some point, we abandon all established structure and support, and we stand alone, no lord to serve, no cause to fight. Being a Ronin provides opportunity to become totally empty. Once we are empty, we can be filled.

I recall, as part of my Ronin journey (a previous part had been stepping out from organized religion), when my marriage dissolved. Maybe you know the hell of a divorce. All illusions of the previous life are suddenly gone. My "stuff" (clothes, canoe, treasures of various sorts gathered across a lifetime) had been retrieved and stored in a friend's South Dakota barn. I had no job. My "home" was a temporary room at a dear friend's house. I received word that the barn had burned and my stuff had vaporized. After the first shock, I laughed and laughed and laughed. I stood naked in the universe, clinging to nothing.

An inner work of the warrior is total abandon. This requires complete trust. Total abandon means being totally present, clinging to nothing, trusting the Source while not clinging even to the trusting. Embodying the immediate current of the Wellspring, allowing the Tao to Tao, God to God, Spirit to Manifest, Emptiness to Form, and Form to Empty.

The inner work of the warrior is to let go of the obscurations of "I, Me, Mine" and of "Want, Don't Want, Don't Care." By allowing these obscurations to dissolve, the warrior opens to and becomes a direct manifestation of Life Force, of Spirit. In this sense he "lays up his treasures in heaven" and "dies before he dies."

Drop Your Story

We are storytellers. Whatever is unknown, we make up stories about. We begin to familiarize it (to bring it into the family). This is one of our gifts as humans. Like all our gifts, it can also become our torment.

We become attached to the story; we begin to see the story as reality. We can "pave paradise" with our stories and "put in a parking lot." We have "paved" the unknown with interpretation, with a story that no doubt is pleasing and satisfying and may even have great predictive value. But it is still just a story.

The torment is the "parking lot." The torment is the solidification of our mind, the hardening of our "ought"-eries, and the "should"-ing all over ourselves. Our mind is made up like a bed in the morning, and we don't want any strange ideas sliding between the covers. We exist in deep trance.

We forget that a story is a story is a story.

A man came in to see me. He told me a torturous story in which he was a victim, the world was unfair. He was alone against the world.

He was right. His story was justifiable. A jury of his peers would not have convicted him. His plight was the fault of others. He was right. And in pain. And stuck, nothing to do but point his finger at his situation.

He finished and sat quietly.

I said, "All of that is just a story."

The silence in the room was deep and long.

He struggled with my statement.

"What do you mean?"

"What you told me is a story. Things happened. What you told me is your story of what happened. You are a victim and there is no way out. As you spoke, a different story came to me describing the same events. I can tell it to you. If you want to hear it."

He wasn't so sure at first. He was slightly stunned at my comments. He may have been expecting commiseration, consolation, sympathy.

More silence.

When he said yes, I told him the story. He was the hero of a journey, rather than the victim of a circumstance. The situation he had described was now one small part of a continuing adventure— the saga of HIM— a saga in which there was no end.

He now had a choice. He could continue to tell himself the victim story, which he had every right to tell, but which would keep him in painful stuckness. Or he could adopt a variation of the story I had told him, which allowed him room to maneuver, to act freely. Or he could drop all stories and simply be here, mindfully present, without describing himself over and over to himself, without putting himself into a trance state of ME and THE STORY OF ME.

No Enemy

Isshinryu karate is a vicious form of in-fighting: bringing the body close to the body of the other and using all the body's hard surfaces (such as fists, knees, elbows, feet, fingers, knuckles) to attack and destroy the soft areas of another's body (such as eyes, throat and neck, armpits, solar plexus, stomach, groin, kidneys). As such, it is one of the "lower" forms of martial arts.

"Lower" means "no harm to me, excessive harm to you." Higher forms of martial arts practice "no harm to me, as little harm to you as possible." The highest arts practice "no harm to me, no harm to you."

The lower arts are relatively easy to learn. Any bozo can destroy. The highest arts can be more difficult. They require a distinct change in attitude, involving a different relationship with fear and anger. The energy of fear and anger remains present, yet fear and anger are nowhere in sight.

This particular shift in worldview is a reason all warriors of spirit—Taoist practitioners, Christian contemplatives, Islamic Sufis, and Buddhist Zen masters—appreciate each other. They live, breathe, and respond as those outside conventional reality. Because there is no enemy, they do not get caught in fear or anger.

They surrender all thought of an enemy. They open to a higher art.

In the Soup

Rumi has a great poem about a chickpea being boiled in a cooking pot. The chickpea takes it personally and tries to leap out. The cook knocks it back in. The chickpea isn't done.

Of course, we are that chickpea. We decide, at times, that we have had enough. We want out now! Getting out in the midst of the process is a half-baked idea. "But the water is too hot!" we cry.

Getting more agitated, we forget about centering and grounding, opening and releasing, fierce intent and compassion (for our own boiling and the boiling of others). We forget that we volunteered for this mission.

We are all in the soup together. Instead of evasion, the warrior cries, "Boil me some more! I'm not done yet!"

Submission

Submission has dual meaning. To submit means to be both active and passive simultaneously. To submit means to yield, to give up; to submit means to hand over, to turn in. We are actively committing to yielding up something, purposely turning something over.

When the word is used in logical argument—such as "I submit to you that the sky is blue"—it means that something is being offered for your consideration. Think of that as con-side-ration: to sit side-by-side with something. When we submit to the principles of the universe (the will of God), we are turning ourselves over to sit side-by-side with these principles, this will. This takes submission. Side-by-side with the universal flux and flow, we begin to move as it does, in accord with it rather than in opposition to it. We enter and blend.

Surrender and submission are acts of courage and trust. We acknowledge that we have emerged (are continuously emerging) from the source (the Living Father, the Ever-Birthing Mother), that we have created our own bubbleheads (secondary reality), and that we shall return (are continuously returning) to the Source. We surrender and submit ourselves to this reality.

Forgiving Is Releasing

Sometimes forgiving is interpreted as letting someone get away with something. We might feel that we want to hold it (their perceived trespass on us) against them for a while, possibly the rest of their lives (and maybe even after). But we are the ones doing the holding—and holding comes with a price. Our souls suffer with bitter anguish.

The holding is within us. The person we are holding something against is probably not affected by it at all. Long-term holding leads to cramp and strain. Unforgiveness is a warping endeavor.

Forgiving is releasing, letting go. What is released? What is let go? The festering sores within our consciousness that we have been nursing so carefully; the clinging sores of resentment, of anger, of hatred, of vengeance. When we forgive, we release ourselves from torment. We allow the wound to heal.

Hands Attaching

A martial practice I have adapted to couples counseling and to work teams is called "hands attaching." The exercise is useful for determining your degree of comfort with surrendering to someone else's lead or whether you must always have *your* way.

It goes like this. Pair off. Stand facing each other with the right foot extended a few inches. Allow the backs of your right hands to touch lightly. That point of contact is where you are having your conversation. One of you will move your hand within the space in front of you, in and out, up and down, right and left. Move smoothly and with full intent. The other of you is to keep your hand attached to the hand of the one who is moving. Breathe naturally. Do not speak. Do this exercise for 3 to 5 minutes.

Notice what happens with the way you feel, what you think, your ability to lead or to follow. Now, continuing verbal silence, reverse roles. The leader now follows wherever the other goes, keeping contact with the other's hand.

Continue for a few minutes.

Discuss what happened. Were you more comfortable leading or following? What were your styles in leading? In following? Forceful? Detached? Jerky? Smooth? Predictable?

Unpredictable? What else? What was communicated each time? Was there a time when you did not know who was following or leading, when your movement merged?

Your Surrendering Practice

One way of surrendering is the practice of humility, of releasing self-importance. To be humble is not necessarily to always put yourself last. That practice can actually be quite self-inflating. To be humble is to release the tight bounds that we are always defending. To be humble is to let go of the bounds, to let go of that all-too-sensitive self-awareness.

What is your surrendering practice? Do you continuously dwell upon you, singing the refrain of I-I-I, me-me-me? When do you drop your story? What is it you need to forgive, to release, to let go? What do you do to open to the Great Capacity?

17

THE WEAPON OF COMPASSION

"The whole creation groans and travails in pain together."

Compassion, at its root (*com* + *pati*), means "to suffer with, to bear with, and to have patience with." Compassion, by necessity, begins with yourself; it begins at the core of your being and extends outward from there. To be compassionate, we cannot evade our own suffering. We are not to wallow in it and cling to it as professional victims, but we are to recognize our suffering and allow it to live its natural life. The only way *out of* suffering is *through* suffering. "Unless a seed falls into the ground and dies, it cannot bear fruit" (John 12:24) is an accurate metaphor for our existence. We are like seeds sown into the ground of the universe.

Imagine a seed in the dark cold ground. The seed may huddle into itself, not wishing to stir, fearful of the great unknown. It fights against any urge to crack its shell (too painful!). Better to stay with the familiar fears and discomfort than to venture out.

Some seeds refuse to open and die fruitlessly.

Those who open begin to reach out toward the light, knowing instinctively the direction. It runs into obstacles: hard rock, at which the opening seed either stops or continues around or through. While it moves toward the light, the seed also begins exploration of the dark by sending roots down into its depth. Eventually the seed opens into the light and finds that along the way it stopped being a seed. In its journey toward the light, it has transformed.

Like fruitful seeds, we suffer with, bear with, and have patience with our own existence and its unfolding. This is compassion.

Entering and Blending

As we practice the eight qualities, we become aware that there are no "others," no beings who are separate from us. Life is an unending web of existence. It is impossible to say where "I" stop and "you" begin. (The attempt to do so has brought a proliferation of attorneys with unceasing argumentation that will continue as long as our co-created secondary reality does not mirror primary reality.)

We become aware that we are not separate from "others" (whether "they" are called humans or plants or animals or earth or molecules or planets, or whatever names we use to designate, to differentiate, to divide and conquer). As we open with compassion for ourselves, we automatically open with compassion for all that is. The whole universe groans with its existence and its unfolding.

But you might want to start small. You might want to have compassion for one other person. Compassion is not pity. Compassion is not misty-eyed romantic sorrow. Compassion requires the use of a certain skill, a certain capability. Compassion requires shape-shifting: the ability to become another, to identify (become identical) with another *without losing your own center*. In martial arts this is known as entering and blending.

Practice of compassion automatically develops our capacity. As we open with compassion, we become roomier. Eventually we have room for the entire universe. As we practice compassion, we lose the concretization of our selves. We become transparent (diaphanous, to use Jean Gebser's term).

Practice of compassion requires fearlessness, refusing to submit to fear. Fearlessness comes from living in primary reality, from having insight into the nature of the universe. We enter into right relationship with all that is. We enter and blend.

Attention and Interbeing

For comprehension of how compassion can lead to an energetic world of open interbeing, consider the following premises:

When attention is given deeply enough, interbeing reveals itself. Interbeing is a term coined by Thich Nhat Hanh to point to the interrelationship of all things. Similar concepts are Indra's Net, wyrd, and the great holoarchy. The point is, the indepth study or deep participation in any field of interest eventually allows us to discern a vast network of interconnection. You might start your study as a particle; you end up as a wave.

Any field of study allows the giving of deep attention. Whatever our field of interest (such as science, music, sports, romance, politics, ecology), we can give it our deep attention. This means more, much more, than "making a living" in that field of interest. This means that our attending is so deep that we *become* the field of interest.

For example, the field of martial art study allows the giving of deep attention. Instead of stopping short and merely learning techniques for defending herself, the true martial artist embodies the principles of the martial arts revealed through the giving of deep attention. Interbeing reveals itself. Persons encountering each other are having a conversation. Like all conversations, martial encounter takes place primarily in the nonverbal realm. *What* is spoken matters less than *how* it is spoken. Martial art or warrior principles are relationship principles, and relationship principles are interbeing principles.

When attention is given deeply enough, we merge with interbeing. Continued identification of self as a separate particle gives way to the realization that all is interbeing, that we are not *the* center of the universe, that we are each *a* center of the universe—in fact, that all other humans are each a center of the universe, that separation does not exist, that all is continuously interconnecting. We relax and merge with interbeing, while still maintaining our own unique centers.

Appreciation

Though you might think of the essence of the way of the martial artist as arrogant destructiveness with total disregard for life and for others, the opposite is true. The nature of the universe is such that the most effective way to deal with aggression is through blending with (having loving-kindness for) those who appear to be the enemy. This is the way of Jesus, of Gandhi, of Martin Luther King, of the Dalai Lama, of Thich Nhat Hahn. This is the way of the highest form of the martial arts. The *essence* of the martial arts is selfless creative harmonious blending with what is.

This necessity for appreciating our "enemy" is in accord with the way the universe works. We are physiologically "wired" for opening to all beings with loving-kindness. A large body of research has shown that appreciation (holding something as precious) produces positive changes within a few minutes in our heart rates, brain rhythms, and immune functions. Feeling appreciation in the area of our hearts produces positive physiological change.

Impeding Compassion

A centuries-old synonym for compassion is "unimpededness." To be compassionate means to exist in clear openness with no blocks, no obscurations, no thing present to impede the natural flowing of the clear light of awareness.

We humans appear to habituate within three major categories of impededness, of inner obscuration, of blocks that disallow compassion. These blocks, which we so assiduously cultivate, serve to reduce us to an inner world of judgmental turmoil. We grow accustomed to this self-induced reduction and come to regard it as "normal."

Our three favorite blocks are Wanting, Not Wanting, and Stupor. I want what I do not have and I cling desperately and with great desire to this wanting. I do not want what I have and I do not want some imaginary possibilities, so I exist in perpetual irritation, even hostility. I prefer to remain ignorant of some things, so I keep myself in a state of stupor.

In addition to the three major blocks, we also cling to three concepts that blind us to a larger reality. The embodying of these three concepts is not only socially approved, but actively encouraged by most of human society. The three blinding concepts are I, Me, and Mine. [*I* am the only one; it's all about *me*; I'll attack you if you bother what is *mine*.]

The three blocks appear necessary when we come at life from the survivor mentality of the "lower" or reptilian brain— and the three concepts appear justified when we come from a perspective of close identification of our "self" with the rooftop chatter of the cerebral cortex.

Perhaps the time has come for a less impeded awareness—an opening to a sense of self much larger than the one we usually entertain.

Giving and Receiving

A practice of great compassion is, while talking with someone who is suffering (emotionally, spiritually, physically) to deliberately and calmly use your breath to receive his pain. Envision his suffering coming into the vastness of your being with your inhalations and disappearing into the fertile void of great capacity. As you exhale, breathe loving-kindness into him. See him surrounded and infused with calm, clear healing energy, with healing light.

During times of meditation or prayer, you might do this for your own being, for others you know, for all life on Earth (including humans), for the planet itself, for the universe. Breathe in all the suffering. Breathe out blessings and loving-kindness.

You may not be able to do this exercise unless you are practiced in the embodying of the Weapon of Great Capacity (see part 7).

Your Compassion Practice

We are led to believe that we are to love ourselves before we can love others. To some extent, this is true. If carried too far, however, we get stuck within a smaller version of ourselves. When we realize the reality of interbeing—that everything rises and falls together, that life is one continuous ebb and flow, that each of us *is* the universe embodying—we can give ourselves permission to love "others" first, to extend loving-kindness to all we meet.

How do you embody compassion in your daily life? What form does your practice of loving-kindness take? What do you hold precious—what do you show appreciation for? Do you enter and blend with people and situations while mindfully maintaining your center? Do you leave a wake of gentleness and healing as you navigate the day? Are you compassionate only to strangers? Are you compassionate only with friends?

What is your compassion practice, O Warrior of Spirit?

Part 6

Horizon Weapons

*The vertical points to relationship with the divine;
we go deep into the earthiness of our being
(centering) and open to the influence of the heavens.
We can be seen as having a "haric line" that extends vertically
from the molten core of the Earth through the hara and heart
and other midline chakras to the far reaches of the heavens.
This is also known as the line of light and as the sword of the spirit.
The horizontal points to the relationships of daily life;
we move from horizon to horizon in the conduct of our daily business.
Two principles/practices allow effectiveness in the horizontal realm.*

18

THE WEAPON OF CALM

Be still as a mountain.

Many of us identify with ceaseless movement and continuous excitation of our minds. Like roving sharks in a sea of jabber, we fear that if we stop, we die. We aim to feel alive through distraction.

Constantly seeking vibratory stimulation, willingly bombarding ourselves with chatter, we devour our lives with "bites" of sound. We frantically sleep in a stuporous soup of undigested bits of nothingness.

Embodying the Earth principles (mindful and centering with relentless intent) and the Heaven principles (opening and surrendering with loving-kindness) produces calmness. We are fully present and at home in the universe.

Being still is not a bad thing. When the going gets tough, the tough get calmer.

Flaming and Drowning

Calm results from deciding to attend to the spark before the flaming (in anger, in ecstasy, in mania). The decision to attend may not be made because the flaming is so addictive. We may decide by default, by not deciding, to keep on flaming. Flaming is a way we have of feeling alive, a destructive way.

What makes you flame? What triggers you into flaming? Who are your flaming role models? Do you go through a periodic flaming as a stress-release method? What is destroyed when you do so?

Calm results from deciding to attend to the tear before the drowning (in sorrow, sadness, and despair). Drowning may be as addictive as flaming. We may recite our litany of woes, our doomsday rosary, and spiral downward into the depths of melancholy. We may have become so skillful that we can do it in nanoseconds. We center in deep gloom.

What makes you drown? What triggers you into drowning? Who are your drowning role models? Do you put yourself through a periodic drowning? Is it a confirmed part of your Spiritual Ineptness Plan? (See the appendix.)

Can you abide being calm? Do you dare?

Patterns of Anger

One inner experience we might consider changing is embodying anger. The body releases adrenaline when we feel threatened: threatened by someone else's words, threatened by the world not being the way we think it should be, threatened by physical danger (and so on).

The *feeling* of anger comes with a release of adrenaline. The *feeling* of anger *is* the rush of adrenaline energy. This energy is neither good nor bad. It just is.

This adrenaline release is really not much of a problem. It just provides a lot of energy. It's what we do with the energy, how we use the energy that can be a problem. At least two patterns of response to the energy of anger are possible: a blind anger pattern and a wisdom pattern.

Blind-Anger Pattern

We can fall into a blind-anger pattern, which may go something like this:

1. Some event occurs. Any event. It doesn't matter.
2. The event gets our adrenaline going.

3. Over the years we have grown to accept the adrenaline release as a signal to nurse feelings of dissatisfaction, frustration, uneasiness, threat, and fear.
4. These feelings are accompanied by thoughts and mental images that have become very familiar to us, so familiar that they seem like "reality."
5. These are thoughts and images of fear, hostility, anger, and hatred.
6. The end of this internal chain of events (the internal chain we have so carefully cultivated over the years because it seemed the only thing we could do) is to feel justified and righteous in declaring the event and all the people involved in the event as our enemy.
7. We either explode with anger or hold it inside (implode).

Explosion. Explosive release, like a nuclear detonation, creates a poisonous wasteland. We may feel better for a moment through the releasing of pressure, but we soon find ourselves living in a self-created hell. Even though we may choose others as the target of our explosive release, the long-range effect is suicidal. We blow up our own world with our anger.

Holding It In (Implosion). We can choose not to release the energy, to hold it in. If we do that for too long, we will implode—explode internally. Implosions can take the form of heart problems, ulcers, bowel irritation, headaches, stomachaches, difficulty breathing, and so on.

Setting ourselves up for an implosion is not a good choice. It's like keeping the top on a pressure cooker without releasing any steam. Something's going to blow. We can safely bet it will be the container of the energy, our physical body. Holding anger energy in over a long period of time is a form of suicide: slow suicide.

To me, these two blind-anger patterns (exploding or imploding) are the most boring choices. I have tried them both. They take no skill or talent. Ho-hum, let's be robots. Have a totally predictable reaction:

event → adrenaline → feelings → thought images → righteousness → explosion / implosion

Ho-hum. Boring choices.

Wisdom Pattern

Rather than reacting like a robot, with our chain pulled by any event that rubs us the wrong way, we might choose to practice a different response.

1. Some event occurs. Any event. It doesn't matter.
2. The event gets our adrenaline going.
3. We regard the adrenaline release as a signal *to move away* from feelings of dissatisfaction, frustration, uneasiness, threat, and fear.
4. We regard the adrenaline release as a signal to *move toward* a mental outlook that allows a calm mind.
5. We immediately practice those methods, producing a calm mind. (These methods, to be described later, are best practiced every day so we will be ready to use them on a moment's notice.)
6. Our calmness of mind allows clear seeing.
7. Clear seeing allows us to act with wisdom.
8. Wisdom means thinking and acting in ways that reduce harm, both the internal harm of implosion and the external harm of explosion.

A wisdom pattern allows us to cultivate positive and strong qualities of mind. The wisdom pattern is:

event → adrenaline → signal to move toward calm → calming mind → clear seeing → acting with wisdom

We become what we practice. Practicing the Wisdom Pattern allows us to transform ourselves into wide-awake, flexible calmness. We no longer fall into the blind trap of anger. Instead, we use anger's energy creatively and constructively.

Waiting

One ingredient of calm is patience. Patience involves abiding by the understanding that wherever you go, *here* you are. "Waiting" is not the same thing as "patient." Waiting is a subjective state, a mental disturbance, a cognitive affliction closely akin to anxiety. Waiting is low-level anxiety.

Patience and compassion co-arise. When we have patience and compassion in a waiting situation (traffic, checkout lines, doctor's offices), we know that everyone is doing the best they can at the moment. Letting go of the judgmental divisive approach produced by the adopted stance of "waiting," we open with calm compassion for what is going on *here*.

When in a "waiting" situation, a warrior of spirit engages in weapons practice: giving and receiving, breathing, posture of unshakable integrity, preparation posture, mindfulness, centering, and so on. A warrior of spirit does not wait. Waiting has disappeared from the menu of possibilities.

Mind Like Moon, Mind Like Water

Martial artists are instructed to have a mind like the moon and a mind like water. These terms point to specific states of consciousness.

A mind like the moon is a mind that serenely reflects the light of Awareness. A mind like the moon does not withhold the light of Awareness from some and reserve it entirely for others. A mind like the moon is a mind that allows clear reflection of Awareness upon everything equally. A mind like the moon is also a mind that exists beyond the intellect, beyond the realm of words. It steadily, consistently, effortlessly allows the light of Awareness to gently unfold to a 360-degree consciousness, shrinking from nothing, opening to all, aware of the seen and the unseen, aware of the tonal and the nagual. The felt experience of mind-like-moon is that of moving into sensing with your whole being, with your body and cells and organs, with your energetic field.

No division exists. No subject. No object. No seer. No seen. Awareness is.

A mind like water is a mind that flows without encumbrance. Water knows no obstacles. It flows under, around, and through. It takes on the shape of all it encounters and yet keeps its own identity, its own qualities. Water does not shy away from anything. It moves with the speed, rhythm, and agility called for by the circumstances. When it encounters hardness, resistance, and density, it flows around with no resistance. When an opening occurs, water flows into and through.

Follow the example of the moon: reflect Reality without reservation. Follow the example of water: know no bounds, no resistance.

No intent. No design. Empty. Yet the moon "sends out" its light. The water "captures" its image. The moon reflects light. The water accurately reflects ever-changing reality with no thought and no effort.

Calm Illumination

A lamp of high intensity sheds more light per square inch than does a less intense light. Intensity refers to the amount of light entering a given space. An intense person is lively and moving with power and energy.

Calmness allows an increase in intensity. Excited intensity is tense. Calm intensity is illuminative. With calm intensity, your mind is like the moon. Your mind is not caught by tension. The light of awareness shines equally on all.

With calm intensity, you have a mind like water. Water flows without interruption or resistance. Water follows the natural contours of existence. Yet water is not passive. The Grand Canyon is an example of water's penetrating power.

Sit in the seat at the center of your soul. Extend awareness in all directions. Express centered awareness. Allow relaxed openness. Move vigorously from a relaxed core.

Mothers and Cousins of Calm

The mother or major prerequisite of calm is the "thorough abandonment" of cognitive affliction. Cognitive affliction can be thought of as clinging to the mind's movies, regarding concepts as real. Cognitive affliction is trembling in fear at your own imagination. To be calm requires no longer entertaining these afflictions, to thoroughly abandon your role as their host.

Calm stillness has no fear. The cousins of calm that produce fearlessness are the other weapons (centering openness, relentless surrendering, mindful compassion, and active engaging). Proficiency in embodying these weapons requires and produces fearlessness. Along the way, we grow calmer.

In-Hell-ing and Ex-Hale-ing

A delightful woman came to see me the other day. She was troubled. She had been holding her spiritual breath. Her in-hale-ation had become an in-*hell*-ation. We all have different ways of doing this. Her way had been to focus on her "self" and her lack of "self"-esteem. Entrancing herself in this way, she was in-hell-ing.

During our time together, she began to laugh about her "self." With her laughter came release. I spoke to her of the sun and how the sun continues radiating, continues exhaling warmth and light no matter what. To ex-"hale" means to send out healthiness (think of it as "hale-thy-ness").

One definition of our (indefinable) Source is that God is a sphere with no surface *whose center is everywhere*. That means that God's center is within each of us. As a center of the universe, our responsibility is to exhale warmth and light from that center. The alternative is to become a continuously inhaling black hole. Meanwhile, we keep the psychotherapists of the world employed.

Word Fasting

From time to time, choose a day and fast from words. (I have found Saturdays to be good days for this.) Do not speak with words from the time of awaking in the morning to going to sleep at night. Let your loved ones know you are going to do this and ask for their cooperation. If you wish, carry a small card that says, "I am not speaking today. I am word fasting. Thanks!"

Enjoy a day of word fasting.

Developing Calm

The following methods for developing calm are part of the training of a warrior of spirit. A warrior of spirit practices embodying and directing Spirit energy, the Life Force that flows through us and gives us being. A warrior sees clearly. Clear-seeing requires calm.

Sitting Still. Sit down. Keep an erect spine. Relax all the muscles not needed to hold up the body. Sit still for 15 to 45 minutes. Do not move. If an itch arises, do not scratch. Simply notice whatever arises. Whatever arises will continue to change.

Breathing. The way we breathe affects our mental state. To calm the mind, focus attention on breathing. Breathe in through the nose slowly, smoothly, and deeply. Breathe out through the mouth. In breathing out, imagine the breath going through all barriers and extending to infinity. Breathe back in. Repeat.

Concentrating. To concentrate means to bring full attention to one thing and keep it there. If the attention goes away, bring it back. You can concentrate on the breath, on an image or a word in the mind, on a picture, on a spot on the wall. Make sure the object of concentration is either neutral or positive.

Everything in the world will arise while concentrating: desire, hostility, pain, fear, fantasies, states of bliss, and so on. If the attention gets caught in them, bring the attention back to breathing. Once uncaught, continue concentrating. While sitting still, allow whatever arises to arise and disappear.

Appreciating. Think of something or someone that you appreciate, that you hold as precious. Sit quietly while feeling that sense of appreciation in the heart area of your chest. Breathe naturally. Sitting quietly while feeling appreciation increases the resistance of the immune system, the heart begins to beat more smoothly and evenly, and the brain waves begin to move in synchrony with the heart.

Moving. Moving around, stretching, flexing, tensing, and releasing allow you to let go of negative feelings. Choose your own way of doing this. It can take any form that suits you. Walking works well.

Embodying. While moving through the day, embody stillness, breathing, concentrating, and appreciating.

Your Practice of Calm

How do you practice calm in your life? Do you keep yourself in a state of agitation? Does silence disturb you? Do you attempt to calm yourself through greater excitation? Can you be with yourself without distractions? Can you be "still as a mountain?"

What calming practices do you embody? Conscious breathing? Yoga? Natural stretching and flexing of muscle groups? Sighs of relief and release? Running? Cleaning house? Going for walks? What is your practice?

19

THE WEAPON OF ACTION

Move like a great river.

Mind, body, and life force move as one. All actions are done with whole heart, with full presence, and with spirit. We fully attend to this, now fully attend to that (which becomes the new this). So-called multitasking, instead of being a frantic division of attention, becomes a quick succession of present moments with full attention to each moment. We are still as a mountain and moving like a great river.

Calling Energy

You can spend much of your time identifying with thoughts and emotions . . . or being a persona (mask) of social fiction

. . . or being a helpless pawn in someone else's game, standing to one side until human life is over . . . or being anything your little heart desires. You can also open to the pure energy of being. You can call for the energy of the universe to flow through you. And it will.

As you begin calling energy, you become less identified with who you are and more identified with the energy of being. By "being," I mean grounding while opening awareness and fluid interplay with what is.

The warrior of spirit learns to "call" energy through certain ways of being. Since universal energy appears inexhaustible and does flow through humans, the warrior works on allowing and encouraging that flow-through. Awareness is focused on whatever blocks the flow, then on evaporating the blockage.

A simple way of energizing is through breathing. All warrior arts emphasize breathing methods in their training. Proper breathing produces heightened energy. Most of the people I see in my profession as a psychologist breathe shallowly, taking little sips of air as if air is highly expensive! When shallowly sipping air, we rob ourselves of free natural energy: oxygen and the oxygenation of the body (including the brain). Inappropriate breathing appears also to be a correlate of depression and anxiety.

Rhythm

Martial arts movements, like the movements of daily interaction with others, vary in rhythm: slow and still movements of long duration; exploding in sudden bursts of energetic expression; weaving and swaying with the unpredictable rhythm of reeds blown in the wind. Martial artists (and conversational artists) follow the rhythm of What Is.

Rhythm, that delightful word of total consonants, refers to "measured and balanced movement." Movement is measured and balanced in two major ways: accent and time value.

In music, notes are often accented (given more emphasis). Accenting changes the rhythm and the experience. For example, experience the difference between the Morse code "Y" and "V." The Morse Y is Dah de Dah Dah and sounds like the old Dragnet theme: Dah de Dah Dah. The V is De De De Dah, accented on the fourth beat, and sounds like the familiar portion of Beethoven's Fifth Symphony: De De De Dah, De De De Dah.

These accentual shifts create a different rhythm with each rhythm producing its own unique mood and experience. Similarly, in the behavioral and martial realm, we shift the rhythm of the interaction through accenting a particular portion of a movement. Accenting is done through allowing a sudden burst of energy at that moment.

In a study of people's responses to the experience of musical rhythms, music-psychologist Alf Gabrielsson found three major experiential categories: structure, motion, and emotion. Structure refers to the experienced pattern of accents and beats. It's the orderly form we create amid the flow of life's current. Motion refers to the perceived rate of the beat. When describing their perception of the motion in music, people in Gabrielsson's study used such descriptors as "walking, dancing, jumping, rocking, swinging, graceful, and driving forward." (Hey! Instead of marching yourself or dragging yourself through the day, how about jumping-rocking-swinging-dancing? Change your beat rate and shift your energy.) Motion is linked with emotion. Gabrielsson reminds us that the intimate bond between motion and emotion is expressed in our everyday language: "one jumps for joy, sinks down in despair, trembles from fear." I'll add struts with pride, expands with happiness, and dances with delight.

In his research, Gabrielsson found that the emotional aspects people described in their experience of rhythm produced the following dimensions: vitality or dullness, excitement or calm, rigidity or flexibility, solemnity or playfulness.

The warrior of spirit moves away from dull, rigid, solemn rhythms and uncentered excitement to vital, calm, flexible, playful, spontaneous unpredictability.

An essential aspect of rhythm is its expressive character. In music, notated (written) rhythm is not the same as played rhythm. The first has no expressive character and merely points to a rhythm to be expressed. The expressive character comes from the liveliness of the musician. That means you! You are the musician, you are the expressive character, and you are the liveliness. How do you want to play it? Vigorous verve? Doldrum dullness? (Maybe you can let *it* play you!)

Body movement expresses rhythm. Look around at folks walking. Each follows a unique rhythm, both reflecting and producing her current emotional state. The sad drag along. The excited bounce. Those in hot pursuit of a chosen goal speed on a direct trajectory.

Playing with the rhythm of your movement in interaction with others can produce in them reactions of tension, relaxation, hesitation, surprise, and joyful expectation. Rhythm's effects are powerful—so choose your rhythms with care. Practice with various rhythms during the day.

Play.

Synchrony

Synchrony means to have the same timing, the same rhythm. Movement toward interpersonal synchrony appears to be a natural process. At a Maui seminar, I invited participants to do the Dah-Dah exercise. It goes like this:

Pair off and face each other, knee to knee. Sit quietly. Let attention go within. Listen for your inner rhythm. What is the rhythm of your inner being at the present moment? Quietly open to the inner sound of dah-dah to accentuate the beat, the pulse, the rate of the internal rhythm. Now sound it out loud while listening to the sounding rhythm of your partner. Become aware of differences, similarities, and possible changes of rhythm over time.

The Maui participants were wondrous folk of differing professions, cultures, and life experiences. The room was flooded with dah-dah sounds, expressions of unique individual rhythm. After a short time, the partners moved to synchrony. Synchrony happened with no conscious effort. Often the merge of partners' rhythms occurred within a third rhythm, previously non-evident.

Participants were uncertain as to how the third rhythm was created. ("I'm not sure if I changed my rhythm or my partner or both of us.") The significance of the third rhythm synchrony was a natural and pleasurable process. Perhaps each human has a characteristic "inner pulse."

Separation Rhythm

The ego is a created set of rhythms based on the illusion of separateness. To become stuck in the ego's rhythms is a serious choice with severe consequences. We become isolated from reality (while all is in relationship at all times).

The rhythm of separate self is the rhythm of fear, of anger, of pride, of desire, of stupor. The fear rhythm is restricted and small (of low amplitude). It has an uneven high amplitude, like the rhythm of a fire with varying amounts of fuel: now burning intensely, now smoldering. The rhythm of pride is a steady inflation, followed by a staccato pop as reality bursts the bubble.

To continuously create the ego illusion—to follow the rhythms necessary for the sustaining of this illusion—requires energy. Not only is the ego addiction an energy drain, it also blinds us to the rhythms of reality, to the actual ebbing and flowing of life.

The Rhythm of Others

When serving as clinical director of a community mental health center, I was called to the reception area. A large man was being verbally aggressive and nonverbally threatening. The man showed signs of escalating, rather than calming, and he seemed to expect confrontation. I stood by the man's side and responded with a slow rhythm of verbal and nonverbal expressiveness. In my inner vision, I did not view the man as an opponent but as a partner in a larger dance—a rhythmic dance of calmness and healing. The man became increasingly calm and was soon able to move out of the reception area to a private room for consultation.

Rhythm, in music, produces a "feeling of regularity ... , a safe ground in the ongoing musical flow." Similarly, your own internal rhythm is your safe ground. You are grounded in your naturally flowing rhythm. To move into the rhythm of another is to move into the other's safe ground. You do not have to give up your own core rhythm while moving into the rhythm of another.

Rhythm also refers to frequency of vibration (and we are vibratory beings). When one vibrational frequency is linked with a similar but not identical frequency, the two will tend to merge into one. If you know how to become attuned to the rhythm of the Larger Context (mostly by becoming still, then opening), you can merge with it. No "enemy" exists. Therefore you can never be overcome or have the need to overcome.

Catching That Free-Flowing Rhythm

He felt stuck in his job. He was bored out of his gourd. I asked: What do you do that is fun? He said (and shifted from pained stuckness to radiant freeness as he spoke): I ride my motorcycle.

As soon as he recalled that free-flowing feeling, he shifted to that way of being. Even though he sat in a chair in my office, nothing was before him but the open road. He decided to practice "riding his motorcycle" through his workday, especially when he saw certain predetermined cues in his office décor, and especially at specific times of day.

You can do the same. Sit quietly and recall what makes you feel alive, filled with enjoyment, free-flowing. Once you re-call, re-collect, and re-member, allow the energy of it to flow through your body. Feel the feeling of it. Set up some cues in your life-space (pictures, images, objects, words). When cued, stop and catch that free-flowing feeling.

Your Action Practice

How do you practice engaging life? What stances do you habitually take? What is your rhythm of the day? How do you deal with the rhythm of others? Are you and your actions synchronous or are "you" usually somewhere else? When walking, are "you" walking? When driving, while talking, while living your life? Are you engaging? Do you engage each moment's situation with your whole being?

How can you be more engaged in your existence? Do you wish to be? Would you rather be in some form of stupor? If so, your action practice might be to deliberately engage in stupor, to be aware of your degree of commitment to stupor, and to remain aware of how well you are being stuporous.

Proficiency in embodying the other warrior weapons (compassion, surrender, opening, mindfulness, relentlessness, centering, and calm) automatically calls forth action. From what actions are you refraining? From what are you holding back? For what are you waiting?

Part 7

The Mystery

Capacity

Confront the lion in his den.
Accept the empty circle.

20

THE TARGET

Early one morning, I began the transition back to earthly life from a lucid dream. Breathing wakefulness into my body, I stretched and flexed. A sentence spoken in the dream resonated in my consciousness with clarity and life-changing power: *Confront the lion in his den; accept the empty circle.* I knew these were life-shaping words. They are written in my heart. They guide my daily life.

I discovered later that the diploma of a graduate of a martial arts school in medieval Japan was a blank sheet with an empty circle. The circle was complete. The martial artist had come full circle. He began knowing nothing. Then he began to know something. Now he truly knows nothing (the place of continuous beginning) as if for the first time.

The graduate of the martial school has followed the path to emptiness. All the techniques, methods and ways are learned, then "forgotten." The graduate warrior becomes a white belt once again. He has beginner's mind: empty of preconceived notions, leaving room for the fullness of universal energy. He *is* the empty circle.

What appears to be a circle from one viewpoint is actually, from another point of viewing, one portion of a continuous spiral. The completed circle is actually one turn of the spiral. The return to the beginning is both a returning and a fresh newness.

As the warrior progresses, emptying may be allowed to occur. Emptying has advantages: one is the ability to take in new information. When I believe or feel I have a firm grasp of reality, I have already lost it. Reality cannot be grasped. Instead of reality, I have grasped a headful of concepts and notions and a bellyful of feelings and desires.

Emptying need not be feared. "Empt" comes from an Anglo-Saxon verb (*amtian*) that means to be at leisure. "Leisure" has its roots in an Old French word that originally meant "permission, opportunity." To be empty is to be permitted, to have license for anything. Someone who is truly emptying is relaxing (at leisure) and is allowing (permitting);

relaxing with the openness of no restriction. That person is on vacate-ion.

"*Amtian*" is composed of two parts: "*ae*" (without, not) and "*metta*" (having to); in others without having to, not having to. When we empty ourselves, we are not filled with "have to," not driven, not loaded, and not burdened. We are not occupied by ego demands. Emptying makes us "poor in spirit"; we count "self" as nothing and thereby gaining "the kingdom of heaven."

Emptying means lightening up, dropping the heavy load of conceptual and emotional baggage, releasing the weight of anxiety, worry, and fear. We realize the openness of interrelation, and we let go of the illusion of the separate "self" with all its problems and demands.

Emptying ourselves allows poise, serenity, and complete assurance. And why not? We have received a continuous "allowance" from the Source of Being. We have freedom within a larger context.

We come from and are continuously being born out of the Great Emptying, the Infinite At-Leisure, the Openness that manifests itself as far and as deep as we can intuit (and further). Nowhere does it abide (stand still). The Great Emptying dances and sings. Out of the Great Emptying, all creation continuously arises.

21

Circum Stance

"Circumstance" refers to all that goes on around (*circum*) the stance or stand we take. The circle that has the ego at its center seeks to attract energy for the ego's purpose; it seeks to pull energy inward toward the center. Universal energy is blocked. When the empty circle is accepted and ego dissolves, the winds of life blow clean through. An empty circle flows with universal energy, with the breath of heaven and earth. The circle is limitless. (It has no bull's "I.")

When I do not accept the empty circle and instead take an ego-stance, I am an excellent target. The ego is like a chip on the shoulder just begging to be knocked off. It's a natural magnet for psychic lightning. The ego forces a separation in the flow of What Is—and in response, life opens to strike the visibly exposed ego. (Something so large and prominent cannot be hidden.)

When ego dissolves and I take the stand of life itself, the stand of the Source of Being, I have confronted the lion within its den. I am accepting the empty circle.

Knotting

Some time ago, I was minding my own business (as usual) when I saw a perfect circle revolving in front of me. I had grown accustomed to this seeing-of-visions, so I knew if someone else were present, they would not see it. As it revolved, it made a sound—*tsst! tsst!*—much like the sound the old vinyl records made when the needle hit a scratch.

"What is that sound?" I silently asked.

"Look more closely," was the instant reply.

I peered more closely. The circle was an unbroken string with a knot in one place. As the string revolved, the knot caused the *tsst!* sound. "What is that knot?" I asked.

"You humans," came the reply. And then I heard a laugh. "You humans are a bunch of knot heads!"

"You mean we stop the universe from running silently and smoothly?"

"Yes."

This cognitive knotting arises from attachment. We become attached to certain movies of the mind. Just as we might enjoy *I Love Lucy* reruns on television, we have our favorite mental shows. They are not always pleasant. We rerun internal movies of guilt, shame, injustices, vengeance. We rerun movies titled *What I Should Have Said* or *If I Could Do It Over Again*. We rerun our fantasies called *Success* or *Failure*.

We also become attached to Thinking. Rather than simply allowing thought to flow through, as a river flows through a landscape, we let ourselves become captured by the river of thought, helplessly swirling in its eddies.

All this creates knots that separate the flow of What Is, knots in the web of existence. We make things convoluted, turned in upon ourselves in a tangled way: a Gordian knot awaiting the single clean sword strike that will release us from illusion.

Re-Form-ing, Re-Bell-ing, and Re-Volt-Ing

Another way we knot is through rebellion and reform. At such times we act as if we are prisoners. We prisoners are always trying to make the prison a better place. We want reform when what we need is revolt. We think there is a warden other than ourselves. We guard ourselves better than any hired mercenary.

We want reform. We want better prison conditions. We wish to remain in prison. We want a better prison: less brutal guards, better food, good medical care, time off for good behavior—but don't take away my prison. Just give me better prison conditions. I want reform. I do not dare revolt.

Revolt does not have to mean violence. Re-volt means to charge from inside, to open to the voltage of the Life Force. Without re-volt, I am a sleepwalking zombie. Without re-volt, I am the living dead.

To re-volt will cost me every thing. To re-volt I must give it all up.

I am the universe universing. I am earth walking. I am sky singing. I do not want re-form and end up in the same shape I've always been. I want re-volt.

Re-volting (opening to energizing spirit) is also different from re-belling. Re-belling is to ring those same old bells, over and over. Re-belling is banging your head against the same old gongs, using you head as the clapper. (What is the sound of one head clapping?)

Only prisoners and slaves re-bell. Free beings re-volt.

"I find you re-volting!"

"Thank you very much!"

Afraid of Nothing

He sat in the chair across from me. Searching for words to describe at least a portion of his deeply felt apprehension (after all, if we can name a beast, it becomes more family-er, less terror-able), he said, "I am afraid of the nothingness that will come if I stop focusing on my thinking."

He habitually identified with his thinking, falling prey to a wild rollercoaster of judgmental emotions and imagery. He knew enough to know that something—sometimes called emptiness or nothingness—emerges as the dominant field when we allow thinking to flow as a subset of consciousness, but he was afraid of the idea of nothingness, of the thought of his self as nothing.

"You mean you are afraid of nothing?" I asked.

His mind vibrated rapidly between the dual meanings, then caught hold. He laughed.

We know how to live in splitness. The realm of the nondual, the not-two, and not-even-one may be less familiar. In fact, most of us go to great lengths to stay out of this realm. We fear it will mean our demise. We may not know, or we may not have experienced, that the non-dual is the Wellspring out of which all arises.

The beginning warrior may start the journey into the maze of existence with full complexity: full of self, ego, and pride (all three are compensations for fear); full of techniques and methods; full of principles and rules. When full of self, we are receptive to nothing else. Our awareness is restricted to buzzing thoughts, self-concerns, emotional states, and our mortal situation. The whole world consists of nothing but "Me, Me, Me."

The Fullness of Emptiness

In late sixteenth- and early seventeenth-century Japan lived an unusual man named Ryokan. To some eyes he seemed a lunatic, a fool, a man of no common sense. He continuously gave away all he had. He voluntarily gave a startled and confused burglar his clothes when the burglar found nothing to steal in his hut—and then he lamented because he could not "give" the burglar the moon. (The burglar had no eyes to see it.)

Nothing could be taken from Ryokan. Owning all, he possessed nothing. So it was also true that nothing could be taken from him. He loved all and was loved in return. When he came around, people lightened up.

Ryokan was a man of cosmic energy. He was re-volting. He swung the sacred sword of Vajraraja, the sword that, according to the story, "cuts and puts to death anything dualistic appearing before it."

All our questions about life and being and the ego with its dualistic and separatist thinking dissolve into Emptiness. As we can see in Ryokan's life, Emptiness is not a dead emptiness. Emptiness allows Spirit flow, life, laughter, love, contentment, energy.

Emptying

One way to empty is through the use of attention. As you sit quietly, pay attention to your thoughts going by. You may see your thoughts as boats on a river or a train with rail cars or as planes taking off and landing. Begin to pay attention to the spaces between the thoughts. At first it may seem as if the spaces are razor thin. However, continue to pay attention to the spaces, the intervals, and they will become larger.

Direct energy to the spaces between thoughts, rather than to the thoughts themselves, and the mind will become positively empty. As the mind empties of preconception and thought, room is allowed for What Is. The mind expands outward to include a subtle sensing of everything. No separation exists.

Great Capacity

The inner work of the warrior of spirit is active daily use of the eight keen weapons, which allows the clearing away of obstructions and obscurations; it opens to the Life Force of the Source; it allows room for Spirit to flow unimpeded.

As with the development of any new skill, at first we may feel clumsy and uncertain when we practice keen weapon use. We may also find that we favor the use of one or two of the keen weapons to the exclusion of others. We may feel greater ease in the practicing of compassion than embodying relentlessness. Or vice versa. This means an imbalance in our warrior skills.

In physical training of warrior ways, we may need to practice twice as much certain movements with our less favored side of the body, be it left or right. Internal spirit training is no different. The complete, well-rounded warrior is skilled in embodying all eight keen weapons.

And what is the target, the aim of this weaponry? The target is depicted by the open spaciousness at the core of the Wheel of Keen Weapons. The target is your own inner core. The weapons are deployed to open space for the expression of the Life Force *through* (and *as*) your moment-to-moment existence.

Embodying the Wheel of Keen Weapons allows great capacity to open. All obscuration dissolves. When you sit in the seat at the center of the soul, the seat disappears and the sitter vanishes. The Wellspring of life itself is your source of energy and action. You are an embodiment of the qualities of the Source: mindfully compassionate; opening and surrendering relentlessly with strong intent; calm, present and active in the continuous emerging of life.

This is the work of the Wheel of Keen Weapons: allowing an opening to the heart of the soul.

Your Practice for Allowing Capacity

There are three practices I have for allowing capacity. One is just sitting, sitting calmly with no agenda other than sitting. A second is walking, especially walking the mountains and canyons of nature. A third is conversing and being with friends (including book friends) of a capacious nature. Capaciousness is catching.

What are your ways? How do you allow capacity in your life? You might sit quietly and reflect upon this for a moment. What are your practices that provide you with capaciousness?

Epilogue

Consider that a metaphor is like a seed. If the seed is planted, watered, nourished, and cultivated, it will grow. Metaphors are explanations (and creators) of reality.

The metaphor being watered in this book is the metaphor of the warrior of spirit. All reality is seen as one vast continuously emerging, perpetually transforming Life Force in which all is mutually interdependent. A warrior of spirit opens and trusts this Life Force.

A cultivator of this metaphor has compassion for all (everything is kin), owns (clings to) nothing, and allows "self" to vanish so Life Force can flow unimpeded.

The embodying of Spirit may seem too fanciful a prospect. If so, it's because of the stance being taken, the continuous identification of the point-from-which-I-view with secondary, rather than primary reality. Secondary reality emerges from and arises out of human fabrication. The world of secondary reality is a world of cognitive structure, of individual and collective belief systems.

These cognitive structures composed of what-I-have-been-told and of what-I-have-learned-so-far and of what-seems-to-work-for-me, are like virtual-reality helmets. With our heads firmly encased, we make moves that are right and proper in relation to our helmet—movements that are out of synchrony with the free-flowing reality of the universe itself.

In the martial and warrior arts, this can get a person injured or killed. Anyone living in virtual reality is a prime target for those who live in primary reality. This is one reason the true martial masters refuse to fight: it wouldn't be a fair fight. (When two dwellers in primary reality meet each other, it is cause for celebration, not hostility.)

In the daily life of human-created reality, wearing a helmet of cognitive obscuration may achieve you a degree of secondary reality success, as long as you associate with others wearing similar helmets (or if you invade groups of other helmet wearers who are less ruthless than you). We naturally seek out others caught up in a virtual reality similar to ours. We believe they see the truth.

A major thesis of this book is that we can catch glimpses of a helmet-free existence—and even live it. In practicing the use of the eight keen weapons, we develop great capacity, naturally opening to the continuous Source-ing of life. We becomes one with the Wellspring. We move in harmony with the Life Force; we blend with the Source. This embodying of Spirit is a natural occurrence.

When a person is unified in mind, body, and spirit, the power of the Life Force is present. When self is forgotten and focus is total, we embody great power. Mothers lift cars off their pinned sons, books and poems are written, mountains are climbed, street hoodlums are chased down the street by grandmas with canes, and societies are transformed. The odds of "normal" reality (in which mind is doing one thing and body is doing another) disappear. The impossible is done.

The invitation is to see for yourself by performing the experiments. You are the scientist, the researcher. The exercises in this book are the experiments. You are the research subject. Perform the experiments. Collect your data. Present your results. Draw your conclusions.

In science, one experiment is not enough. In fact, experimentation never stops. Scientists build on a body of research produced by themselves and other members of the scientific community. In a similar way, the embodying of Spirit is a research area with vast amounts of data collected over centuries by scientists from many cultures. This book is one summation of that data, with specific focus on the wisdom developed by masters of hand-to-hand combat.

The universe is our natural home. The universe breathes us, calls us into being at every moment. The specific daily life practice (the inner work) of the warrior, outlined in this book, gives us the tools we need so that each and every one of us can live as warriors of spirit. The inner work of the warrior is the embodying of Spirit.

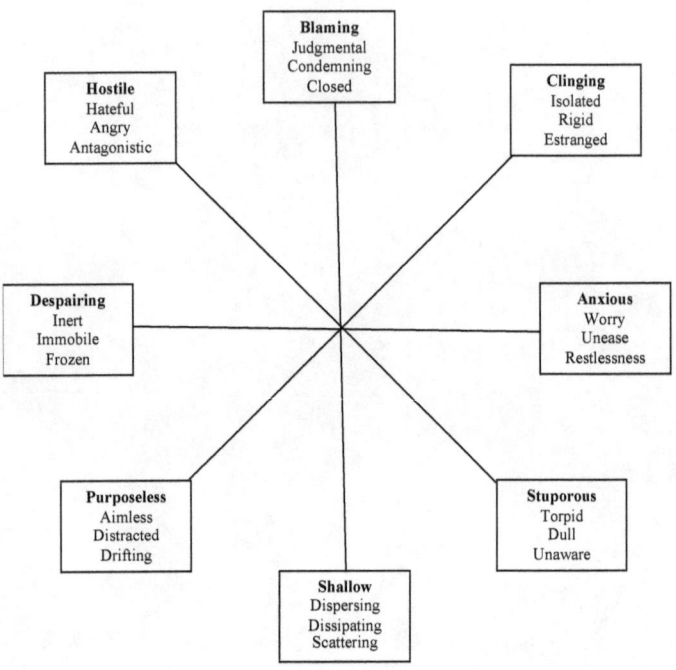

**The Wheel of Ineptness:
Practices Promoting
Spiritual Death**

Appendix:
The Wheel of Ineptness

The Wheel of Ineptness is absolutely essential if you wish to develop a comprehensive Spiritual Ineptness Plan (SIP), allowing you to sip at life, rather than participating fully by drinking deeply from its wellsprings. The Wheel depicts the efficiency of a SIP. If you embody any one of the eight practices, the other seven will soon follow.

Notes and Additional Reading

Part 1. My Personal Journey

Additional Notes on Chapter 2, The Martial Journey

For a list of the martial arts principles, take a look at Patrick McCarthy's *The Bible of Karate: Bubishi* (Tuttle, 1995, pp. 159-160).

Sensei Shimabuku's English translation of these principles, as presented on my graduation silks, are:

1. A person's heart is the same as heaven and earth.
2. The blood circulating is similar to the sun and the moon.
3. The manner of drinking and spitting is either hard or soft.
4. A person's unbalance is the same as a weight.

5. The body should be able to change direction at any time.
6. The time to strike is when the opportunity presents itself.
7. The eye must see all sides.
8. The ear must listen in all directions.

For more on Ki, read *Book of Ki: Co-Ordinating Mind and Body in Daily Life* by Koichi Tohei (Tokyo: Japan Publications, 1962, 1973, 1974, 1976, and 2001).

Here is a list of the spiritual writings I studied during this time: The Bible; the Gospel of Thomas; the Bhagavad Gita; the Dhammapada; the Diamond Sutra; the Qur'an; the Tao Te Ching; the I Ching; the writings of Patanjali, Meister Eckhart, Santideva, Black Elk, Hakuin, Dogen, Hui-Neng, Alan Watts, Rumi, Ibn 'Arabi, Sri Aurobindo, Gandhi, Thomas Merton, Bede Griffiths, Chogyam Trungpa, Bernadette Roberts, and Thich Nhat Hanh.

Additional Notes on Chapter 3, The Professional Journey

In case you're interested, here's a list of my professional writing during this time:

Breed, George, "The Effect of Intimacy: Reciprocity or Retreat?," *British Journal of Social and Clinical Psychology* 11 (1972): 135-142.

Breed, G., Christiansen, E., and Larson, D., "The Effect of a Lecturer's Gaze Direction Upon His Teaching Effectiveness," *Journal Supplement Abstract Service* 2, Ms. 226 (1972).

Breed, G, and Porter, M., "Eye Contact, Attitudes, and Attitude Change Among Males," *Journal of Genetic Psychology* 120 (1972): 211-217.

Breed, G. and Colaiuta, V., "Looking, Blinking, and Sitting: Nonverbal Dynamics in the Classroom," *Journal of Communication* 24 (1974): 75-81.

Naiman, T.H. and Breed, G., "Gaze Duration as a Cue to Judging Conversational Tone," *Representative Research in Social Psychology* 5 (1974): 115-122.

My experience in therapeutic relationships came due to the following professional roles: chief psychologist of a four-county system of behavioral health clinics in southeastern Arizona; clinical director of an outpatient team of psychologists and counselors for a northern Arizona behavioral health system (Flagstaff, Williams, and Page); and staff psychologist for the Employee Assistance and Wellness Office of Northern Arizona University.

I gained experience in the field of healing as the creator and teacher of courses for the University of South Dakota School of Medicine; teacher of therapeutic touch courses to staff of South Dakota hospitals and clinics; and co-developer of and presenter in statewide wellness programs.

The direct experiences that overlapped with my quest for information are sometimes called "mystical," though there is nothing "misty" about them. Politics, business, and the entire realm of human consensual reality is more ephemeral than is the Ground of Existence forming the world, that which creates and sustains the universe beyond human creation. Co-creation with the Source is everlasting; co-creation with humans rises and disappears.

Part 2. The Mandala: The Wheel of Keen Weapons
Additional Reading

Dharmaraksita, *The Wheel of Sharp Weapons: A Mahayana Training of the Mind*, Library of Tibetan Works and

Archives (Indraprastha Press, Nehru House: New Delhi, 1981).

Friday, Karl with Seki Humitake, *Legacies of the Sword: The Kashima-Shinryu and Samurai Martial Culture* (Honolulu: University of Hawaii Press, 1987).

Gleason, William, *The Spiritual Foundations of Aikido* (Rochester, VT: Destiny Books, 1995).

I Ching: Book of Changes, 17th printing, the Richard Wilhelm Translation rendered into English by Cary F. Baynes (New York: Bollingen, 1980).

Panikkar, Raimundo, *The Vedic Experience* (Berkeley: University of California Press, 1977).

Sato, Hiroaki, trans., *The Sword and the Mind* (Woodstock, NY: Overlook, 1986).

Stevens, John, *The Essence of Aikido* (Tokyo: Kodansha, 1999).

Trungpa, Chogyam, *Training the Mind and Cultivating Lovingkindness* (Boston: Shambhala, 1993).

Underhill, Evelyn, *Practical Mysticism* (New York: Dutton, 1943).

Wallace, B. Alan, *Buddhism with an Attitude: The Tibetan Seven-Point Mind Training* (Ithaca, NY: Snow Lion Publications, 2003).

Additional Notes on Chapter 4, The Wheel of Keen Weapons

I am indebted to Dharmaraksita, composer of *The Wheel of Sharp Weapons*, to its translation across the centuries from Sanskrit to Tibetan into English (Indraprastha Press, Nehru House: New Delhi, 1981), and to Cynthia Knox for bringing this text to my attention. Though the wheel I use arose from the warrior qualities depicted in the martial and spiritual arts, I have adapted its title from the work of Dharmaraksita, for the existence of which I am deeply grateful.

Structural use of an octogram to display universal principles has been employed by others:

1. The Fivefold Law of hand-to-hand combat and Eight Divine Coordinates of Kashima-Shinryu show, in their depiction of "spiritual martial power" that the martial arts are a path for engaging the divine in daily living (Friday and Humitake, 1997).
2. Book II of Richard Wilhelm's translation of the *I Ching* gives a reference to and depiction of Fu Hsi's octagonal arrangement leading to the development of the 64 hexagrams of the *I Ching*. Not only was the structure and form an octogram similar to the Wheel of Keen Weapons, but the content was similar enough to be regarded as further validation.
3. The Eight Powers of Shinto are diagrammed and described by Osensei Ueshiba, founder of Aikido (Stevens, 1999) and by William Gleason (1995).
4. Raimundo Panikkar (1977) gives a drawing of a spoked "wheel of the cosmos" with earth depicted below and heaven above from the Rig Vedas.
5. The eight-spoked wheel is an age-old symbol of Buddhism.

What Jesus called the kingdom of heaven and many have referred to as supernatural, I am calling primary reality and unitive consciousness. Separative consciousness (secondary reality) is the sickness that has beset us. Unitive consciousness (primary reality) is the antidote, the healing.

Separative consciousness involves experienced awareness of a distinct, seemingly unbridgeable distance between self and others, experiencing self as a particle rather than a wave (to use a physics metaphor), experiencing others as objects (I-It relationships), and engaging in behavior that promotes social isolation. Separative consciousness experiences the world as profane ("outside the temple"), as not sacred.

Unitive consciousness involves being in relationship with everyone and everything, feeling at home in the universe, being deeply grounded and centering while open to all that exists, experiencing self and others (including so-called insentient beings) as kin (I-Thou relationships), experiencing oneself as a "wave" rather than a particle, engaging in behavior that promotes social harmony, and experiencing the world as sacred.

A subset or forerunner of unitive consciousness, relationship consciousness (comprehending the systemic nature of life, that everything is in relation), is both an area of practice and a vehicle for moving toward and opening to unitive consciousness.

Separative and unitive consciousness can be seen as anchoring the ends of a dimension or continuum:

Separative  Unitive

As such, a person's consciousness state is generally in flux on that dimension. A given person's consciousness state may habitually occupy one portion, one range of that dimension, while some persons may habitually exist in separative consciousness. Others may have unitive consciousness as their general state. Still others may fluctuate between the two depending on their current situation. Embodying the qualities depicted in The Wheel of Keen Weapons moves one toward unitive consciousness

Part 3. The Metaphor: Warriors of Spirit
Additional Reading

Bolelli, Daniele, *On the Warrior's Path: Philosophy, Fighting, and Martial Arts Mythology* (Berkeley, CA: Frog, 2003).

Chitwood, Terry, *How to Defend Yourself Without Even Trying* (Sioux Falls, ND: Polestar, 1981).

Dear, John, *Jesus the Rebel: Bearer of God's Peace and Justice* (London: Sheed and Ward, 2000).

Deshimaru, Taisen, trans. Nancy Amphoux, *The Zen Way to the Martial Arts* (New York: Arkana, 1982).

Fauliot, Pascal, *Martial Arts Teaching Tales of Power and Paradox* (Rochester, VT: Inner Traditions, 2000).

Furuya, Kensho, Kodo, *Ancient Ways: Lessons in the Spiritual Life of the Warrior / Martial Artist* (Santa Clarita, CA: Ohara, 1996).

Gichin, Funakoshi, *Karate-Do Kyohan: The Master Text* (Tokyo: Kodansha, 1973).

———, *Karate-Do: My Way of Life* (Tokyo: Kodansha, 1975)

Hyams, Joe, *Zen in the Martial Arts* (Los Angeles: Tarcher, 1979).

Jou, Tsung Hwa, *The Tao of Tai-Chi Chuan* (Warwick, NY: Tai Chi Foundation, 1991).

Leggett, Trevor, *Zen and the Ways* (Boulder, CO: Shambhala, 1978).

McCarthy, Patrick, trans., *The Bible of Karate: Bubishi* (Boston: Tuttle, 1995).

Musashi, Miyamoto, translated by Bradford Brown, Yuko Kashiwagi, William Barrett, and Eisuke Sasagawa, *The Book of Five Rings: Gorin No Sho* (New York: Bantam, 1982).

Nitobe, *Inazo, Bushido: The Warrior's Code* (Burbank, CA: Ohara, 1979).

Payne, Peter, *Martial Arts: The Spiritual Dimension* (New York: Thames and Hudson, 1981).

Ralston, Peter, *Cheng Hsin: The Principles of Effortless Power* (Berkeley: North Atlantic, 1999).

Shi Ming, with Siao Weijia, translated by Thomas Cleary, *Mind Over Matter: Higher Martial Arts* (Berkeley, CA: Frog, 1994).

Skoss, Diane, ed., *Koryu Bujutsu: Classical Warrior Traditions of Japan* (Berkeley Heights, NJ: Koryu Books, 1997).

Stevens. John, *The Secrets of Aikido* (Boston: Shambhala, 1995).

——, *The Philosophy of Aikido* (Tokyo: Kodansha, 2001).

Takuan Soho, translated by William Scott Wilson, *The Unfettered Mind: Writings of the Zen Master to the Sword Master* (Tokyo: Kodansha, 1988).

Tohei, Koichi, *What Is Aikido?* (Tokyo: Rikugei, 1962).

Wilson, William Scott, trans., *Budoshoshinshu: The Warrior's Primer of Daidoji Yuzan* (Santa Clarita, CA: Ohara, 1984).

Additional Notes on Chapter 7, The Monk-Warrior Metaphor

Beverly Lanzetta, PhD, introduced the term "social mystic" into my vocabulary in her August 2003 seminar on Theologies of Nonviolence at Northern Arizona University, in which she adroitly led an eclectic group in studying the theology and spiritual practice that guided some of the twentieth century's greatest social mystics, among them M. K. Gandhi, Martin Luther King, Jr., Abraham Joshua Heschel, Thomas Merton, Dorothy Day, and Thich Nhat Hanh.

The phrase "direct intuitive observation," comes from Alfred North Whitehead, quoted in David Ray Griffin's Re-enchantment without *Supernaturalism: A Process Philosophy of Religion*. (Cornell University Press, 2001), page 54.

I see parallels between the concepts of "monk-warrior" and "social mystic." Though the phrases may evoke differing imagery ("monk-warrior" seems more vividly individualistic, condensed, and focused; "social mystic" seems more generic of the species, widespread, and open; "monk-warrior" seems more a rushing stream, while "social mystic" seems more a flood plain), at base they are remarkably similar, if not the same.

An Additional Note on Chapter 10, The Sacred and the Profane

"Bodhisattva" can be translated as "spiritual being," "spiritual warrior," or "awakening warrior." *Awakening*, because the person who takes the vows of a bodhisattva continues to open awareness. An awakening warrior lets go of fixed concepts and ideas (*idée fixe*: a form of insanity), releases rigid definitions of self as a permanent unchanging entity, allows ongoing expansion of awareness, and allows consciousness to open outside the realm of cognition. *Warrior*, because the bodhisattva faces all that arises. She is a spiritual emergency medical technician. He practices and uses skillful means in helping others stop their emotional and conceptual bleeding, prevent the shock of separate-self illusion, and heal the wounds that come with clinging and attaching. For more on this, see Red Pine's translation of *The Diamond Sutra* (Counterpoint, 2001).

An Additional Note on Chapter 11, Warriors of Spirit

I first encountered this process of disidentification through having but not being attached through reading Roberto Assagioli. See his *The Act of Will* (The Synthesis Center, 2010).

Additional Reading for Chapter 12, The Weapon of Centering

Crum, Thomas F, *Journey to Center* (New York: Simon & Schuster, 1997).

Griffiths, Bede, *Return to the Center* (Springfield: Templegate, 1976).

Haruo Yamaoka, *Meditation Gut Enlightenment: The Way of Hara* (San Francisco: Heian, 1976).

Heckler, Richard, *Holding the Center: Sanctuary in a Time of Confusion* (Berkeley, CA: Frog, 1997).

Roberts, Bernadette, *The Path to No-Self: Life at the Center* (Albany: State University of New York, 1991).

Von Durckheim, *Karlfried Graf. Hara: The Vital Centre of Man* (London: Unwin Paperbacks, 1984).

Part 4. Earth Weapons

Additional Reading

Arrien, Angeles, *The Four-Fold Way: Walking the Paths of the Warrior, Teacher, Healer, and Visionary* (New York: Harper, 1993).

Castaneda, Carlos, *The Wheel of Time: The Shamans of Ancient Mexico, Their Thoughts About Life, Death and the*

Universe (New York: Washington Square Press, 1998).

Coelho, Paulo, *Warrior of the Light* (New York: HarperCollins, 2003).

Leonard, George, *The Way of Aikido: Life Lessons from an American Sensei* (New York: Dutton, 1999).

Lowry, Dave, *Autumn Lightning: The Education of an American Samurai* (Boston: Shambhala, 2001).

Mushima, Yukio, translated by Kathryn Sparling, *The Way of the Samurai: Yukio Mishima on Hagakure in Modern Life* (New York: Perigree, 1983).

Neville, Robert C., *Soldier, Sage, Saint* (New York: Fordham University Press, 1978).

Parry, Danaan, *Warriors of the Heart* (Cooperstown, NY: Sunstone, 1989).

Reid, Howard and Michael Croucher, *The Way of the Warrior: The Paradox of the Martial Arts* (London: Leopard, 1995).

Rinchen, Geshe Sonam, *The 37 Practices of Bodhisattvas* (Ithaca, NY: Snow Lion, 1997).

Santideva, translated by Kate Crosby and Andrew Skilton, *The Bodhicaryavatara* (New York: Oxford, 1996).

Santideva, translated by Vesna Wallace and Alan Wallace, *A Guide to the Bodhisattva Way of Life* (Ithaca, NY: Snow Lion, 1997).

Trungpa, Chogyam, *Shambhala: The Sacred Path of the Warrior* (Boulder, CO: Shambhala, 1984).

Tsunetomo, Yamamoto, *The Hagakure: A Code to the Way of the Samurai* (Tokyo: Hokuseido, 1980).

Wright, Craig, *The Maze and the Warrior* (Cambridge, MA: Harvard University Press, 2001).

An Additional Note on This Section:

To read more about the "sensual immersion in nature," see David Abram's *The Spell of the Sensuous: Perception and Language in a More-Than-Human World* (Vintage, 1997).

Additional Notes on Chapter 13, The Weapon of Mindfulness

To read more on the practice of living fully in the present moment, see Jon Kabat-Zinn's *Full Catastrophe Living* (Delacorte, 1990) and his *Wherever You Go, There You Are* (Hyperion, 1994).

Jean-Luc Marion develops the idea of the eye becoming dull, stuck on a single viewpoint, when we are judgmental in his *God Without Being* (Thomas A Carlson, trans., University of Chicago Press, 1995).

Regarding the Chiltan Posture: archeologists have found ancient markings that depict human figures standing in a certain posture. In *The Four-Fold Way: Walking the Paths of the Warrior, Teacher, Healer, and Visionary* (HarperOne, 1993), Angeles Arrien speaks of this standing posture combined with hand positions as a warrior empowerment tool. Angeles does not say which hand goes where, though her two accompanying drawings show each way (one shows right hand over heart, the other show left hand).

Additional Reading on Mindfulness

Hanh, Thich Nhat, *The Miracle of Mindfulness: A Manual on Meditation* (Boston: Beacon Press, 1987).

Kabat-Zinn, Myla and Jon Kabat-Zinn, *Everyday Blessings: The Inner Work of Mindful Parenting* (New York: Hyperion, 1998).

Salzberg, Sharon, *A Heart as Wide as the World: Living with Mindfulness, Wisdom, and Compassion* (Boston: Shambhala, 1997).

Additional Notes on Chapter 14, The Weapon of Relentless Intent

To read more about Isshinryu, see Trevor Leggett's *Zen and the Ways* (Shambhala, 1978), page 136. The drawing of a warrior on horseback is on page 194.

Thanks to Sensei Koichi Tohei for the exercise given under "Mind and Body as One."

Additional Reading on Relentless Intent

Assagioli, Roberto, *The Act of Will* (New York: Penguin, 1973).

Strozzi-Heckler, Richard, *In Search of the Warrior Spirit: Teaching Awareness Disciplines to the Green Berets* (Berkeley, CA: North Atlantic, 2003).

Shosan, Suzuki, translated by Arthur Braverman, *Warrior of Zen: The Diamond-Hard Wisdom Mind of Suzuki Shosan* (Tokyo: Kodansha, 1994).

Stevens, John, *The Sword of No-Sword: Life of the Master Warrior Tesshu* (Boulder, CO: Shambhala, 1984).

Part 5. Heaven Weapons

An Additional Note on Chapter 15, The Weapon of Opening

For more on opening to sense others, see Abram's *The Spell of the Sensuous: Perception and Language in a More-Than-Human World*.

Further Reading on Opening

De Caussade, Jean-Pierre, translated by John Beevers, *Abandonment to Divine Providence* (New York: Image Books, 1975).

Fenelon, *Let Go* (Springdale, IL: Whitaker House, 1973).

Mann, John and Lar Short, *The Body of Light: History and Practical Techniques for Awakening Your Subtle Body* (New York: Globe Press, 1990).

Metzner, Ralph, *Opening to Inner Light: The Transformation of Human Nature and Consciousness* (Los Angeles: Tarcher, 1986).

Additional Notes on Chapter 16, The Weapon of Surrendering

For more on surrendering the "carcass" so that it can be rendered, see Michael Harner's *The Way of the Shaman* (HarperCollins, 1980).

Jesus spoke of being an outlaw—like a Ronin, someone who is outside the established boundaries—in a passage that is seldom mentioned: "He said to them [his disciples], 'When I sent you out barefoot without purse or pack, were you ever short of anything?' 'No,' they answered. 'It is different now,' he said; 'whoever has a purse had better take it with him, and his pack too; and if he has no sword, let him sell his cloak to buy one. For scripture says, 'And he was counted among the outlaws,' and these words, I tell you, must find fulfillment in me; indeed, all that is written of me is being fulfilled.' 'Look, Lord,' they said, 'we have two swords here.' 'Enough, enough!' he replied" (Luke 22: 35-38).

In Matthew 6:20, Jesus talks about laying up treasures in heaven. To read more about "dying before you die," see Bawa

Muhaiyaddeen, *To Die Before Death: The Sufi Way of Life* (The Fellowship Press, 1997).

For a beautiful and moving rendition of the distinction between the story of pain, the narrative of pain, and pain itself, see Sharon Cameron's *Beautiful Work: A Meditation on Pain* (Duke University Press, 2000).

Further Reading on Surrendering

Barks, Coleman, trans., *The Essential Rumi* (New York: HarperCollins, 1995).

Additional Notes on Chapter 17, The Weapon of Compassion

Romans 8:22 speaks of the groaning of creation.

Regarding compassion and the martial arts, one of the most powerful martial artists who ever lived, Morihei Ueshiba, wrote:

> The martial arts are not concerned with brute force to knock opponents down, nor with lethal weapons that lead the world into destruction. The true martial arts, without struggling, regulate the ki of the universe, guard

the peace of the world, and produce and bring to maturity everything in Nature. Therefore, martial training is not training that has as its primary purpose the defeating of others, but practice of God's love within ourselves.

For more on how appreciation changes us physically, see Rollin McCraty's work at the Institute of HeartMath (www.heartmath.org).

The exercise I suggest in which you breathe in the world's suffering and breathe out blessing is a version of the Tibetan practice known as Tonglen. To learn more about Tonglen, see Ken Wilber's *Grace and Grit* (Shambhala, 2001), Allan Wallace's *The Seven-Point Mind Training* (Snow Lion, 2004), and Chogyam Trungpa's *Training the Mind and Cultivating Loving-Kindness* (Shambhala, 2003).

Further Reading on Compassion

Gebser, Jean, translated by Noel Barstad with Algis Mickunas, *The Ever-Present Origin* (Athens: Ohio University Press, 1985).

Davidson, Richard and Anne Harrington, eds., *Visions of Compassion: Western Scientists and Tibetan Buddhists Examine*

Human Nature (New York: Oxford University Press, 2002).

Fox, Matthew, *A Spirituality Named Compassion and the Healing of the Global Village, Humpty Dumpty and Us* (San Francisco: Harper and Row, 1979).

Gyeltsen, Geshe Tsultim, *Compassion: The Key to Great Awakening* (Boston: Wisdom Publications, 1997).

Hanh, Thich Nhat, *Teachings on Love* (Berkeley, CA: Parallax, 1998).

Salzberg, Sharon, *Lovingkindness: The Revolutionary Art of Happiness* (Boulder, CO: Shambhala, 1997).

Stevens, John, *The Art of Peace: Teachings of the Founder of Aikido* (Boston: Shambhala, 1992).

Part 6. Horizon Weapons

A Note on This Section

To read more about the haric line, read Barbara Brennan's *Hands of Light* (Bantam Doubleday, 1993). Trevor Leggett speaks of the line of light in his *Realization of the Supreme Self*

(Kegan Paul, 1995). The "sword of the spirit" is referred to in Ephesians 6:17.

An Additional Note on Chapter 18, The Weapon of Calm

For more on "thorough abandonment," see Geshe Gedun Lodro's *Calm Abiding and Special Insight: Achieving Spiritual Transformation Through Meditation* (translated by Jeffrey Hopkins, Snow Lion, 1998).

Additional Notes on Chapter 19, The Weapon of Action

To learn more about being still as a mountain while moving like a river, see *The Essence of Tai Chi Ch'uan* by Benjamin Lo, et al. (North Atlantic, 1986).

Quotations on people's responses to rhythm come from a remarkable article, "The Complexities of Rhythm," by Alf Gabrielsson of Uppasala University, Sweden. The article appeared in *Psychology and Music: The Understanding of Melody and Rhythm* edited by Thomas J. Tighe and W. Jay Dowling (Lawrence Erlbaum Associates 1993), pages 93–120.

George Leonard writes about our inner pulse in *The Silent Pulse* (Bantam, 1981).

To use the words of Aaron Copland to describe our ability to catch a free-flowing inner state: "All you need do is to relax, letting the rhythm do with you what it will" (*What to Listen for in Music* [McGraw-Hill, 1939]).

Part 7. The Mystery: Capacity

An Additional Note on Chapter 20, The Target: Great Capacity

In Matthew 5:3, Jesus says, "Blessed are the poor in spirit, for theirs is the kingdom of heaven."

Additional Notes on Chapter 21, Circum Stance

You can read the story about Ryokan in John Stevens' *Three Zen Masters: Ikkyu, Hakuin, Ryokan* (Kodansha, 1993) and in *Ryokan: Zen Monk-Poet of Japan*, translated by Burton Watson (Columbia University Press, 1977). D. T. Suzuki describes the blind burglar in *Zen and Japanese Culture* (Bollingen, 1973), page 365.

Further Reading on Capacity

Abram, David, *The Spell of the Sensuous* (New York: Vintage, 1996).

Anthony, Dick, Bruce Ecker, and Ken Wilber, eds., *Spiritual Choices: The Problem of Recognizing Authentic Paths to Inner Transformation* (New York: Paragon House, 1987).

Batchelor, Stephen, *Verses from the Center: A Buddhist Vision of the Sublime* (New York: Riverhead, 2000).

Carse, James, *Finite and Infinite Games* (New York: Ballantine, 1987).

Forman, Robert K. C., *The Innate Capacity: Mysticism, Psychology, and Philosophy* (New York: Oxford University Press, 1998).

Gallegos, Stephen, *The Personal Totem Pole* (Santa Fe, NM: Moon Bear Press, 1990).

Guyon, Jeanne, *Experiencing the Depths of Jesus Christ* (Auburn, CA: Christian Books, 1975).

Halevi, Z'ev ben Shimon, *Kabbalah: Tradition of Hidden Knowledge* (New York: Thames and Hudson, 1998).

Hanh, Thich Nhat, *Transformation at the Base: Fifty Verses on the Nature of Consciousness* (Berkeley, CA: Parallax Press, 2001).

Harding, D. E., *On Having No Head* (New York: Arkana, 1986).

Housden, Roger, *Fire in the Heart: Everyday Life as Spiritual Practice* (London: Element, 1991).

Leggett, Trevor, *Realization of the Supreme Self* (New York: Kegan Paul, 1995).

Leonard, George, *The Silent Pulse: A Search for the Perfect Rhythm That Exists in Each of Us* (New York: Dutton, 1978).

Lerner, Michael, *Spirit Matters: Global Healing and the Wisdom of the Soul* (Charlottesville, VA: Hampton Roads, 2000).

Macy, Joanna, *World as Lover; World as Self* (Berkeley, CA: Parallax, 1991).

Macy, Joanna, *Mutual Causality in Buddhism and General Systems Theory: The Dharma of Natural Systems* (Albany: State University of New York, 1991).

Marion, Jean-Luc, translated by Thomas Carlson, *God Without Being* (Chicago: University of Chicago Press, 1995).

Red Pine, *The Diamond Sutra: the Perfection of Wisdom*, text and commentaries translated from Sanskrit and Chinese (New York: Counterpoint, 2001).

Sinetar, Marsha, *Ordinary People as Monks and Mystics* (New York: Paulist, 1986).

Wilber, Ken, *The Eye of Spirit: An Integral Vision for a World Gone Slightly Mad* (Boston: Shambhala, 1997).

Additional Notes on the Epilogue

A common metaphor of our society is the metaphor of the market, where all reality is seen as one vast marketplace. Use of this metaphor ("buying" into it) restricts reality to marketers (sellers), the marketed (products), and the marketees (buyers or consumers). The seed of this metaphor is being watered every day. Many have devoted their lives to watering this seed. The metaphor itself is being "sold" globally.

Some of us, for various reasons, may be closet helmet wearers. We may be able to adopt other helmet realities during the day, but in our private spaces, we wear a different helmet. Some of us may note that such a notion as the embodying of Spirit may not be in our helmet repertoire, or, if it is, it is seen as spacey, ethereal and otherworldly; in other words, not real. Some of us may decide that we are happy with the helmet we have and do not wish to be disturbed.

All of us are embodyings of Spirit (Life Force) at all times. Otherwise we would not exist. If you truly think that you are separate from, outside this force, you have become a demigod, a little god unto yourself. You have become super-natural, removed from the natural.

For a martial art example of unification of mind, body, and spirit, see George Leonard's *The Silent Pulse*, the chapter: "This Isn't Richard." Another example is portrayed in *The Return of the King*, the third film in The Lord of the Rings trilogy. Frodo is bound and in danger of death in a tower room. Sam, his friend, is rushing up the stairs to save him despite three monster warriors in his way. According to the arts of war, Sam has every disadvantage: he is occupying the low ground and fighting upward; he is small in size; he is outnumbered; he is relatively unskilled in weaponry; his opponents are large, muscular, skilled, and ruthless. None of that matters. Sam plows right through them with relentless intent. His mind and body are moving in perfect accord with a single purpose: to free his friend. As a result he is an embodying of Spirit.

Further Reading on Topics Within This Book

Awareness and Insight

De Mello, Anthony, *Awareness: The Perils and Opportunities of Reality* (New York: Doubleday, 1990).

Deng, Ming-Dao, *Scholar Warrior: An Introduction to the Tao in Everyday Life* (New York: HarperCollins, 1990).

Fox, Matthew, *Meditations with Meister Eckhart* (Santa Fe, NM: Bear and Company, 1982).

Goldstein, Joseph, *The Experience of Insight* (Boulder, CO: Shambhala, 1987).

Hanh, Thich Nhat, *Being Peace* (Berkeley, CA: Parallax, 1987).

———, *The Blooming of a Lotus* (Boston: Beacon, 1997).

Kornfield, Jack, *A Path With Heart: A Guide Through the Perils and Promises of Spiritual Life* (New York: Bantam, 1993).

Norbu, Namkhai, translated by John Shane, *Dzogchen: The Self-Perfected State* (London, UK: Arkana, 1989).

Purce, Jill, *The Mystic Spiral: Journey of the Soul* (New York: Thames & Hudson, 1980).

Rabinowitz, Ilana, ed., *Mountains Are Mountains and Rivers Are Rivers: Applying Eastern Teachings to Everyday Life* (New York: Hyperion, 1999).

Salzberg, Sharon, ed., *Voices of Insight* (Boulder, CO: Shambhala, 1999).

Thurman, Robert, *Inner Revolution* (New York: Penguin, 1999).

Trungpa, Chogyam, *Cutting Through Spiritual Materialism* (Boulder, CO: Shambhala, 1987).

Underhill, Evelyn, *The Spiritual Life: Great Spiritual Truths for Everyday Life* (Oxford, UK: Oneworld, 1993).

Watts, Alan, *The Wisdom of Insecurity* (New York: Vintage, 1968).

Common Ground

Aronson, Martin, ed., *Jesus and Lao Tzu: The Parallel Sayings* (Berkeley, CA: Seastone, 2000).

Borg, Marcus, ed., *Jesus and Buddha: The Parallel Sayings* (Berkeley, CA: Ulysses Press, 1997).

Davies, Stevan, trans., *The Gospel of Thomas* (Woodstock: Skylight Paths, 2002).

Griffiths, Bede, *The Marriage of East and West* (Springfield, IL: Templegate, 1982).

Griffiths, Bede, *A New Vision of Reality: Western Science, Eastern Mysticism and Christian Faith* (Springfield, IL: Templegate, 1990).

Hanh, Thich Nhat, *Living Buddha, Living Christ* (New York: Riverhead, 1995).

———, *Going Home: Jesus and Buddha as Brothers* (New York: Riverhead, 1999).

Schuon, Frithjof, *The Transcendent Unity of Religions* (Wheaton, IL: Quest, 1993).

Wilber, Ken, *The Marriage of Sense and Soul: Integrating Science and Religion* (New York: Random House, 1998).

Contemplative Psychology

Benoit, Hubert, *The Supreme Doctrine: Psychological Encounters in Zen Thought* (New York: Inner Traditions, 1984).

Brazier, David, *Zen Therapy: Transcending the Sorrows of the Human Mind* (New York: Wiley, 1995).

De Wit, Han, translated by Marie Louise Bard, *Contemplative Psychology* (Pittsburgh, PA: Duquesne University Press, 1991).

———, *The Spiritual Path: An Introduction to the Psychology of the Spiritual Traditions* (Pittsburgh, PA: Duquesne University Press, 1999).

Fromm, Erich, D. T. Suzuki, and Richard De Martino, *Zen Buddhism and Psychoanalysis* (New York: Harper and Row, 1970).

May, Gerald, *Will & Spirit: A Contemplative Psychology* (San Francisco: Harper & Row, 1982).

Molino, Anthony, ed., *The Couch and the Tree: Dialogues in Psychoanalysis and Buddhism* (New York: North Point, 1998).

Reynolds, David, *Playing Ball on Running Water* (New York: Quill, 1984).

Watts, Alan, *Psychotherapy East and West* (New York: Mentor, 1963).

Welwood, John, *Toward a Psychology of Awakening* (Boston: Shambhala, 2002).

Wilber, Ken, *Integral Psychology: Consciousness, Spirit, Psychology, Therapy* (Boston: Shambhala, 2000).

Evolution of Consciousness

Beck, Don and Christopher Cowan, *Spiral Dynamics: Mastering Values, Leadership, and Change* (Cambridge, MA: Blackwell, 1996).

Bucke, Richard, *Cosmic Consciousness: A Study in the Evolution of the Human Mind* (New York: E.P. Dutton, 1969).

Chaudhuri, Haridas, *The Evolution of Integral Consciousness* (Wheaton, IL: Quest, 1977).

Feuerstein, Georg, *Structures of Consciousness: The Genius of Jean Gebser* (Lower Lake, CA: Integral Publishing, 1987).

Gebser, Jean, translated by Noel Barstad with Algis Mickunas, *The Ever-Present Origin* (Athens: Ohio University Press, 1985).

Redfield, James, Michael Murphy, and Sylvia Timbers, *God and the Evolving Universe: The Next Step in Personal Evolution* (New York: Tarcher, 2002).

Underhill, Evelyn, *Mysticism: A Study in the Nature and Development of Man's Spiritual Consciousness* (New York: New American Library, 1974).

Wade, Jenny, *Changes of Mind: A Holonomic Theory of the Evolution of Consciousness* (Albany: State University of New York, 1996).

Embodying

Berger, K. T., *Zen Driving* (New York: Ballantine, 1988).

Claremon, Neil, *Zen in Motion: Lessons from a Master Archer on Breath, Posture, and the Path of Intuition* (Rochester, VT: Inner Traditions, 1991).

Hanna, Thomas, *Bodies in Revolt: A Primer in Somatic Thinking* (Novato, CA: Free Person Press, 1970).

Herrigel, Eugen, *Zen in the Art of Archery* (New York: Vintage, 1971).

———, *The Method of Zen* (New York: Vintage, 1974).

Kepner, James, *Body Process: Working with the Body in Psychotherapy* (San Francisco: Jossey-Bass, 1993).

Kurtz, Ron and Hector Prestera, *The Body Reveals: An Illustrated Guide to the Psychology of the Body* (New York: Harper and Row, 1976).

Murphy, Michael, *The Future of the Body* (Los Angeles: Tarcher, 1993).

——— and Rhea White, *The Psychic Side of Sports* (Reading, PA: Addison-Wesley, 1978).

Palmer, Wendy, *The Intuitive Body: Aikido as a Clairsentient Practice* (Berkeley, CA: North Atlantic Books, 1994).

Smith, Edward, *The Body in Psychotherapy* (Jefferson, NC: McFarland, 1985).

Stevens, John, *The Marathon Monks of Mount Hiei* (Boston: Shambhala, 1988).

Strozzi-Heckler, Richard, *The Anatomy of Change: East/West Approaches to Body/Mind Therapy* (Boston: Shambhala, 1984).

———, ed., *Being Human at Work: Bringing Somatic Intelligence into Your Professional Life* (Berkeley, CA: North Atlantic, 2003).

Energy / Life Force / Ki / Spirit

Chuen, Lam Kam, *The Way of Energy: Mastering the Chinese Art of Internal Strength with Chi Kung Exercise* (New York: Fireside, 1991).

Hiew, Chok C, *Energy Meditation: Healing the Body, Freeing the Spirit* (New York: toExcel, 1999).

Homma, Gaku, *Aikido for Life* (Berkeley, CA: North Atlantic Books, 1990).

Liao, Waysun, *T'ai Chi Classics* (Boston: Shambhala, 1990).

Liu Hua-Yang, translated by Eva Wong, *Cultivating the Energy of Life* (Boston: Shambhala, 1998).

Lo, Benjamin, Martin Inn, Robert Amacker, and Susan Foe, *The Essence of Tai Chi Ch'uan* (Berkeley, CA: North Atlantic, 1986).

Tohei, Koichi, *How to Develop Ki* (Tokyo: Ki No Kenkyukai, 1973).

———, *How to Unify Ki* (Tokyo: Ki No Kenkyukaim, 1974).

———, *Book of Ki: Coordinating Mind and Body in Daily Life* (Tokyo: Japan Publications, 1976).

———, *Ki in Daily Life* (Tokyo: Japan Publications, 2001).

Wildish, Paul, *The Book of Ch'i* (Boston: Tuttle, 2000).

Yang, Jwing-Ming, *Tai Chi Secrets of the Ancient Masters* (Boston: YMAA Publication Center, 1999).

Yuasa, Yasuo, translated by Shigenori Nagatomo and Monte Hall, *The Body, Self-Cultivation, and Ki Energy* (Albany: State University of New York Press, 1993).

Meditation

Aron, Elaine and Arthur Aron, *The Maharishi Effect: A Revolution Through Meditation* (Spokane, WA: Stillpoint, 1986).

Austin, James, *Zen and the Brain: Toward an Understanding of Meditation and Consciousness* (Cambridge, MA: MIT Press, 1999).

Chagme, Karma, *Naked Awareness: Practical Instructions on the Union of Mahamudra and Dzogchen* (Ithaca, NY: Snow Lion. 2000.

De Mello, Anthony, *Sadhana: A Way to God* (New York: Image, 1984).

Dossey, Larry, ed., *The Power of Meditation and Prayer* (Carlsbad, CA: Hay House, 1997).

Goldsmith, Joel, *Beyond Words and Thoughts* (Secaucus, NJ: Citadel, 1968).

Goleman, Daniel, *The Meditative Mind: The Varieties of Meditative Experience* (New York: G.P. Putnam, 1988).

Ibn 'Arabi, *Journey to the Lord of Power: A Sufi Manual on Retreat* (Rochester, VT: Inner Traditions, 1989).

Johnston, William, *Silent Music: The Science of Meditation* (New York: Perennial, 1976).

——, ed., *The Cloud of Unknowing* (New York: Image, 1996).

Keating, Thomas, *The Human Condition: Contemplation and Transformation* (New York: Paulist Press, 1999).

Kongtrul, Jamgon, translated by Sarah Harding, *Creation and Completion: Essential Points of Tantric Meditation* (Boston: Wisdom, 1996).

Merton, Thomas, *Spiritual Direction and Meditation* (Collegeville, MN: The Liturgical Press. 1960).

Pennington, Basil, *Centering Prayer: Renewing an Ancient Christian Prayer Form* (New York: Image, 1982).

Taimni, I. K., *The Science of Yoga* (Wheaton, IL: Quest, 1972).

Tarrant, John, *The Light Inside the Dark: Zen, Soul, and the Spiritual Life* (New York: Harper, 1998).

Wallace, B. Alan, *The Bridge of Quiescence: Experiencing Tibetan Buddhist Meditation* (Chicago: Open Court, 1998).

Whitehill, James, *Enter the Quiet: Everyone's Way to Meditation* (New York: Harper & Row, 1980).

Wood, Ernest, *Concentration: An Approach to Meditation* (Wheaton, IL: Quest. 1981).

Transformation of Society

Autry, James and Stephen Mitchell, *Real Power: Business Lessons from the Tao Te Ching* (New York: Harper, 1998).

Bahro, Rudolf, *Avoiding Social and Ecological Disaster: The Politics of World Transformation* (Bath, UK: Gateway Books, 1994).

Cobb, John B, Jr., *Transforming Christianity and the World* (Maryknoll, NY: Orbis, 1999).

Heider, John, *The Tao of Leadership* (Atlanta, GA: Humanics, 1986).

Hershock, Peter, *Reinventing the Wheel: A Buddhist Response to the Information Age* (Albany: State University of New York, 1999).

Kamentzky, Mario, *The Invisible Player's Consciousness as the Soul of Economic, Social, and Political Life* (Rochester, VT: Inner Traditions, 1999).

Laszlo, Ervin, *The Age of Bifurcation: Understanding the Changing World* (Philadelphia, PA: Gordon & Breach, 1991).

Laszlo, Ervin, *Macroshift: Navigating the Transformation to a Sustainable World* (San Francisco: Berrett-Koehler, 2001).

Loy, David, *The Great Awakening: A Buddhist Social Theory* (Boston: Wisdom, 2003).

Macy, Joanna and Molly Young Brown, *Coming Back to Life: Practices to Reconnect Our Lives, Our World* (Gabriola Island, BC: New Society, 1998).

Zen

Dogen, Eihei and Kosho Uchiyama, translated by Thomas Wright, *Refining Your Life: From the Zen Kitchen to Enlightenment* (New York: Weatherhill, 1990).

Dogen, Eihei, translated by Shohaku Okumura and Taigen Daniel Leighton, commentary by Kosho Uchiyama Roshi, *The Wholehearted Way* (Boston: Tuttle, 1997).

Foster, Nelson and Jack Shoemaker, eds., *The Roaring Stream: A New Zen Reader* (New York: Ecco, 1996).

Kasulis, T. P., *Zen Action / Zen Person* (Honolulu: University Press of Hawaii, 1985).

Sahn, Seung, *Dropping Ashes on the Buddha* (New York: Grove, 1994).

———, *The Compass of Zen* (Boston: Shambhala, 1997).

Sokei-an, Mary Farkas, ed., *The Zen Eye: A Collection of Zen Talks by Sokei-an* (New York: Weatherhill, 1993).

Stevens, John, *Three Zen Masters: Ikkyu, Hakuin, Ryokan* (Tokyo: Kodansha, 1993).

Suzuki, D. T., *Zen and Japanese Culture* (Princeton, NJ: Princeton University Press, 1970).

Suzuki, Shunryu, *Zen Mind, Beginner's Mind* (New York: Weatherhill, 1972).

Uchiyama, Kosho, translated by Shohaku Okumura and Tom Wright, *Opening the Hand of Thought* (New York: Arkana, 1993).

Watson, Burton, trans., *Ryokan: Zen Monk-Poet of Japan* (New York: Columbia University Press, 1977).

ABOUT THE AUTHOR

Photo by Naima Schuller.

George Breed began intensive training in the martial arts (Isshinryu Karate) while serving in the United States Marine Corps on Okinawa in 1959. Upon returning to the states, he taught karate and jujutsu in Atlanta, Georgia, and in Gainesville, Florida.

After receiving his doctorate in psychology from the University of Florida in 1969, and being taught Ki principles by Aikido Sensei Koichi Tohei in 1974, George began teaching workshops on the application of martial arts principles to daily life. He has taught these principles and practices to health professionals (hospital and outpatient); fire fighters; behavioral health staff; county and state government workers; members of Native American nations in Arizona, South Dakota, North Dakota, and Nebraska; university faculty members and staff; Elderhostel members; and attendees of state wellness programs, as well as international conferences.

George lives in Flagstaff, Arizona, and is an avid hiker of the mountains and canyons of northern Arizona, southern Utah, and Colorado. He was born in the Year of the Tiger.

MORE BOOKS BY GEORGE BREED

**The Hidden Words
of the Living Jesus:
A Commentary on
the Gospel of Thomas**
Author: George Breed
Price: $19.99
Paperback
Ebook Available
272 pages
ISBN: 978-1-937211-88-2

With his trademark earthy exuberance, author George Breed explores the deep meanings within the Gospel of Thomas, giving readers new and surprising insights into the message of Jesus.

"The Gospel of Thomas is emerging as a true mystical source from the earliest period of what became Christianity. Any commentary on Thomas is worth reading—but this one is a genuine gem!"
—**Fr. Richard Rohr, O.F.M.**, Center for Action and Contemplation, Albuquerque, New Mexico

"In this lovely book, Dr. George Breed helps to advance the art of seeing, not what rests on surfaces but rather that which lies through and beyond exteriors and forms, and within ourselves."
—**Bradley Olson, Ph.D.**, Jungian Depth Psychologist

Jesus and Lao Tzu: Adventures with the Tao Te Ching
Author: George Breed
Price: $14.95
Paperback
Ebook Available
236 pages
ISBN: 978-1-62524-107-8

"How can I describe this book? If I say it is brilliant, crazy, hilarious, sobering, vulgar, and sublime, all those words are true—but they are certainly not enough to express the contents of Jesus & Lao Tzu. The book defies being categorized or neatly summarized. It will have to suffice if I say simply this: the book's words make me happier, freer, and wiser. If you read it with an open heart, I predict it will do the same for you."

–Kenneth McIntosh, author of *Water from an Ancient Well: Celtic Spirituality for Modern Life.*

Heart of Meditation: Interflow
Author: George Breed
Price: $14.95
Paperback
Ebook Available
226 pages
ISBN: 978-1-62524-256-3

In this paperback collection of the e-book series titled Meditations of the Heart, the author offers bite-size entries into mindfulness and transformation. Each meditation could be used as a vehicle for greater consciousness—or as a prayer leading to deeper awareness of spiritual reality and being. One Amazon reviewer summarized: "Each tiny gem of a meditation holds meaning beyond and beneath the words, and each provides nourishment for the mind and the heart. Concise, simple, but packed with a powerful load of thought-provoking enlightenment, George Breed gives more to us in his meditations with a dozen or so words than most philosophers give in twelve dozen."

Anamchara Books
Books to Inspire
Your Spiritual Journey

In Celtic Christianity, an *anamchara* is a soul friend, a companion and mentor (often across the miles and the years) on the spiritual journey. Soul friendship entails a commitment to both accept and challenge, to reach across all divisions in a search for the wisdom and truth at the heart of our lives.

At Anamchara Books, we are committed to creating a community of soul friends by publishing books that lead us into deeper relationships with God, the Earth, and each other. These books connect us with the great mystics of the past, as well as with more modern spiritual thinkers. They are designed to build bridges, shaping an inclusive spirituality where we all can grow.

To find out more about Anamchara Books and order our books, visit **www.AnamcharaBooks.com** today.

Anamchara Books
Vestal, New York 13850
www.AnamcharaBooks.com

www.ingramcontent.com/pod-product-compliance
Lightning Source LLC
LaVergne TN
LVHW041627060526
838200LV00040B/1471